PROFILES OF THE FIRST WORLD WAR

THE SILHOUETTES OF CAPTAIN H.L. OAKLEY

JERI

IN ASSO

MARY EVAN͡S͡ ͡ ͡ ͡ ͡URE LIBRARY

Have you been Silhouetted?

Capt. Oakley's Silhouettes are world-famous. Cut out direct without any previous drawing a perfect likeness is guaranteed in a few minutes.

Children's full-length Portraits make novel presents which are always appreciated.

Come and see the Artist at work.

Bentalls Ltd
KINGSTON-ON-THAMES

BOOK DEPARTMENT — GROUND FLOOR

© H.L. Oakley Collection/Mary Evans Picture Library (HLOC/ME)

First published 2013
by Spellmount, an imprint of

The History Press
The Mill, Brimscombe Port
Stroud, Gloucestershire, GL5 2QG
www.thehistorypress.co.uk

© Jerry Rendell, 2013

The right of Jerry Rendell to be identified as the Author
of this work has been asserted in accordance with the
Copyright, Designs and Patents Act 1988.

British Library Cataloguing in Publication Data.
A catalogue record for this book is available from the British Library.

ISBN 978 0 7524 9352 7

Typesetting and origination by The History Press
Printed in Great Britain

Contents

Harry Lawrence Oakley, 1882–1960. (HLOC/ME)

Preface

The idea for this book can be traced back to Barbara Philpott who has an encyclopaedic knowledge of the Oakley family and a strong gift of friendship. Her meticulous research and the shining enthusiasm with which she wrote it up were the inspiration for the book. We both have roots in the Oakley family and I had inherited a large amount of material from my maternal grandmother's generation, much of it relating to her brother Harry Lawrence Oakley.

Luci Gosling got the book under way. Oakley's silhouettes were published in *The Bystander* and other magazines now in her care at the Mary Evans Picture Library. She had written her own book, *Brushes & Bayonets*, about artists and the First World War, and saw the potential for a book about Oakley. She passed the idea to Joanna de Vries at The History Press who took it up. Making the book was a challenge because I wanted Oakley's material to tell his story with the minimum of authorial intervention. It required a precise integration of text and images with little scope for moving them about to get the pagination right. Joanna and Paul Baillie-Lane, along with their designer colleagues, have succeeded brilliantly.

My sister, Sally Courage, and cousins, Christopher Rolfe and Margaret Rowe, have allowed me to use Oakley material in their possession. Oakley was prescient enough to ask his family to keep all of the letters he sent home during the war. Setting them with his sketches and photographs, alongside his silhouettes, takes us as close as possible to being there.

My wife Anne encouraged and sustained me throughout the project, including long periods when I was effectively absent from home; and she corrected most of the grammatical infelicities to which I am prone. My son, Alex, and daughter, Amanda Gibbon, patiently instructed me in systems management and rescued me from many glitches and crashes.

I am grateful to several friends who have contributed in various ways, including dating material and allowing me to try out passages on them. Robin Davis took me on two memorable trips to the battlefields, which considerably enriched my understanding of what went on there. In that context, I would like to pay tribute to the Commonwealth War Graves Commission for the outstanding work they do. It is humbling to find new names being added to memorials and old names being re-engraved all the time. They really will live for evermore.

Since I started researching the book some years ago I have discussed Oakley's work with several professional people in the field. The warmth of their appreciation of his talent came as a surprise and added greatly to my enthusiasm for the project.

8TH BATTALION

THE GREEN HOWARDS

I am enormously grateful to Major General Andrew Farquhar for writing the foreword. It is an honour to Oakley's memory and fully in keeping with the regimental saying 'Once a Green Howard always a Green Howard'. I am grateful too for much help and friendliness from the staff at the Green Howards Museum in Richmond, North Yorkshire.

Thank you all very much for helping to make the book. It has been a privilege to put it together.

Jerry Rendell OBE
Windsor, 2013

Foreword

As a Green Howards officer I am delighted to write this foreword to Jerry Rendell's book. A century after the start of the First World War, the Army and society need to be reminded of what regimental life was all about and this book does just that. This is particularly important for today's Army as they undergo yet another review which could sap morale, motivation and camaraderie. Lawrence Oakley joined the Yorkshire Regiment, the Green Howards and he would recognise these regimental names and their immortal spirit today. These enduring links are so important in sustaining a regiment's fighting spirit and the selfless commitment of officers and soldiers over the years. Jerry Rendell's interpretation of Lawrence Oakley's war work throws a spotlight on history that will help us all to understand these timeless ingredients that make up the very soul of the Army today.

Lawrence Oakley MBE was a remarkable artist, and a fine officer in the Green Howards. He was born in 1882 the son of a successful businessman in Yorkshire, but of Shropshire farming stock. From an early age he demonstrated a natural ability to make shapes with scissors and black paper, which his mother recognised and encouraged. His early life saw him making a living from teaching art and cutting silhouettes to order from his studios in Yorkshire. His wider artistic talent was demonstrated when he joined the interior design team for the Peace Palace in The Hague and by the fact he has twenty-three significant silhouettes in the National Portrait Gallery.

But in late 1914, with the clouds of war gathering, Lawrence did not hesitate to cast aside his art career and set off towards the breaking storm. He was commissioned into the 8th Battalion the Yorkshire Regiment, the Green Howards. This was a regiment full of gutsy Yorkshiremen to whom Lawrence could relate; it was a regiment he came to love, to call his own and which featured on his gravestone.

After commissioning, this enthusiastic second lieutenant found himself on the Western Front, at Armentières on the Somme. He became a popular and successful young officer, seeing some of the principal actions of the First World War. He was appointed as an aide de camp to the General Officer Commanding the 32nd Division and saw further action elsewhere in France and Italy, prior to returning to France in early 1918 in time for the German Spring Offensive and the Allies' response of the Hundred Days Offensive. To his surprise throughout these war years he found time to create remarkable silhouettes of his colleagues at arms, and subjects to tell his own story of the war.

As an officer in the Green Howards, his rural background and Yorkshire upbringing stood him in good stead. He was able to relate well to his fellow officers, his Yorkshire soldiers, the local French, even the Germans, and especially the horses of war. Lawrence combined his artistic skills with his professional knowledge as an officer, to capture the manner in which officers and soldiers conducted themselves, both in the trenches and at home on leave.

Jerry Rendell has carefully selected some key pieces of Lawrence Oakley's work and used them to give the reader a very real understanding of what life at war was like for the Army and society at large. You will find the book difficult to put down, which is a testament to Jerry Rendell's empathy and insight into what Lawrence Oakley was trying to portray. He has managed to interpret the true meaning of each cut of the black paper that formed these masterpieces. But such a talent to interpret these works should not come as a surprise when you realise that Jerry Rendell is Lawrence Oakley's sister's grandson. He appears to have inherited Lawrence Oakley's ability to interpret the atmospherics of war, but through a different medium and at a different time.

Jerry Rendell has produced a masterful piece of work, which is a must for anyone who wishes to understand the finer points of soldiering during the First World War, but also with an enduring relevance to today.

Major General Andrew Farquhar CBE DL
President of the Green Howards' Association, Deputy Colonel the
Yorkshire Regiment and Chairman of the Green Howards' Museum
Board of Trustees

Introduction

Lawrence Oakley was one of the most talented and prolific silhouette artists of the twentieth century. He began his career just before the First World War and continued almost until his death in 1960. He enlisted soon after Britain entered the war in August 1914 and while he was waiting to begin his training he designed a recruiting poster, which was also used in Australia and, with different wording, in Canada.

He was then commissioned by the Admiralty to design a poster for the Royal Navy and his image was again used in Canada, in both English and French. The two posters made his name as an artist and opened the way for him to get his work published during the war. He sent material to *The Bystander* magazine whenever he could and they published it under the general heading 'Trench Life in Silhouette'.

Oakley cut his silhouettes from black paper using a small pair of scissors and worked very quickly, so he could combine his silhouette work with his army duties. As well as showing scenes in and around the front line he cut hundreds of portraits of fellow officers. He didn't charge for them and they were very popular as mementos to send home. His best-known portrait was of the Prince of Wales, taken while he was visiting the troops in Belgium.

He served in the 8th Battalion of the Yorkshire Regiment (the Green Howards) then held various staff posts, including a year as the ADC to a General. This gave him a wider range of experience and access to information that would not normally be the lot of a junior officer. As well as his silhouettes this book uses his drawings, photographs and letters home, together with other documents that he retained, to tell his story of the war.

After the Armistice he served in Bonn as part of the British Army of Occupation of the Rhineland, and *The Bystander* continued to cover events there for some years. Oakley was demobilised in May 1919 but continued to illustrate the columns from England.

After the war he travelled around Britain working in resort towns – especially Llandudno in North Wales – in summer, and in London and Edinburgh during the winter. He took around 100,000 portraits and had a large commercial practice doing advertisements for many leading companies including the London Underground, the London and North Eastern Railway, Selfridges, the International Stores, Lee & Perrins and Fenwicks. As well as *The Bystander*, his silhouettes were published in the *Graphic*, *Holly Leaves*, the *Ladies Field*, the *Illustrated Sporting and Dramatic News*, *London Opinion*, the *Orbit* and other titles.

Oakley was well known and highly regarded in his time and for some years afterwards but is largely forgotten today. In the 2005 'Silhouettes' exhibition at the National Portrait Gallery there were three of his portraits but that was a rare showing. This book brings together enough of Oakley's work to tell his story of the First World War and to give an idea of the range and quality of his work afterwards.

Chapter 1

The Making of a Silhouette Artist

Lawrence Oakley aged 4 and his sister, Margaret,
the author's grandmother. (HLOC/ME)

Moat Farm at Stapleton near Shrewsbury. A pen and ink drawing by Lawrence
Oakley's brother, Richard Oakley. (Jerry Rendell (JR))

Lawrence Oakley came from a branch of the Oakley family which had been established in Shropshire for several hundred years and which is still strongly represented there. His grandfather, Robert Brazenor Oakley, was the tenant of Moat Farm, part of the Powys estate. Lawrence's father, Robert Henry Oakley, was born there in 1845 but the late 1840s were very hard times for farmers in England and in 1849 Lawrence's grandfather had to sell up and leave the land.

As the eldest son, Robert Henry might have expected to take over Moat Farm but instead he was sent to be apprenticed to a pharmacist in Liverpool. When he completed his apprenticeship he moved to Yorkshire but retained strong ties with Shropshire. His unmarried sister, Miss Emma Oakley, lived in Buttington near Welshpool. Robert Henry took his children there for holidays and as adults, Lawrence and his brothers visited Emma regularly until her death in 1915.

The inscription on Lawrence Oakley's headstone describes him as being 'of Yorkshire and Salop'.

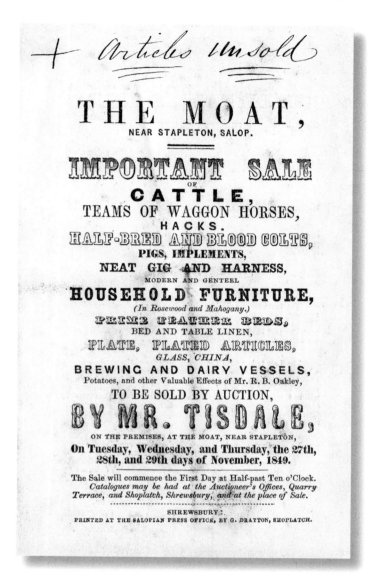

Sale notice for the disposal of Robert Brazenor Oakley's effects. (JR)

An idea of the harshness of the economic conditions for farmers can be gained from the results of the sale. There were 87 lots of livestock, all of which sold. Most of the 313 lots of household furniture and domestic items sold. Not one of the 63 lots of farm machinery and equipment sold.

The final Moat Farm Account 1850 – Liabilities. (JR)

After selling all his goods and chattels and all the produce from the farm, Lawrence's grandfather, Robert Brazenor Oakley, raised £956 10s 7d, but his liabilities were £1,016 6s 10d, of which £839 11s 6d was owed in rent to the Powys estate. It was a Dickensian situation.

The final Moat Farm Account 1850 – Assets. (JR)

To avoid being declared bankrupt he borrowed enough money from two local men to enable him to pay off his debts and to set up in business as a merchant selling coal and other bulk goods. As security, he and his wife signed over the rights to all future legacies they expected to receive. Fortunately the new business was successful.

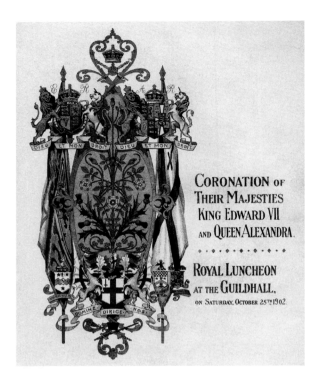

Invitation to attend the coronation of King Edward VII,
1902. (JR)

When Robert Henry Oakley finished his apprenticeship he moved to York and set up in business there. He eventually ran two chemist shops, one in Coney Street in the centre of the city and one further out on the Fulford road. He became an Alderman of the city and, along with the Lord Mayor, represented York at the coronation of King Edward VII and Queen Mary.

Robert Henry Oakley married Mary Elizabeth Dresser, a distant cousin of the designer Dr Christopher Dresser, and they had five children.

Harry Lawrence Oakley was born at Poppleton, near York, on 28 December 1882, the middle child. His father Robert Henry had been named Robert for his father, Robert Brazenor, but to avoid confusion was always called Henry or more familiarly, Harry.

Harry Lawrence was named for his father, but again to avoid confusion was always called Lawrence or Lawrie in the family and among friends. Although Lawrence remained his preferred style throughout his life he was called Harry by some of his contemporaries. This book uses Lawrence.

A page from Oakley's childhood scrapbook. (JR)

Lawrence Oakley started to cut out figures from scraps of paper from an early age. His mother saw his natural talent and bought him black paper and some loose pages of silhouettes for him to copy.

Silhouettes by Mr Brierly of Rochdale. (JR)

Above is one of the pages of silhouettes which Lawrence's mother bought for him. Brierly was a mill worker from Rochdale so cutting silhouettes was presumably just a hobby or a sideline. Lawrence's copy of Brierly's mare and foal is in the centre of the page opposite.

Under the monkey he has written 'Allan' (correct spelling Alan), the name of his eldest brother. That would have been done in the late 1880s when the controversy over Charles Darwin's theory of evolution was still very much alive. Even a 7-year-old might have picked up on it and used it as an excuse to be cheeky about his brother.

A page from a scrapbook which Oakley later annotated 'Early work about 7 yrs old'. (JR)

A poster for the Leeds School of Art, 1905. (HLOC/ME)

A modelling class at the Royal College of Art. Oakley is on the left. (JR)

As well as his skill at cutting out, Lawrence was also good at drawing. His artistic ability was recognised at his local school and he was transferred to the York School of Science and Art and then to the Leeds School of Art. From there he won a free studentship and a county bursary, which enabled him to attend the Royal College of Art in London, where he was awarded his ARCA diploma in 1908.

'The Art Master in the Art Room'. Oakley at the Royal
Grammar School, Worcester. (JR)

After he left the Royal College of Art, Oakley decided to take up teaching. He worked first for the London County Council as a Special Instructor of Drawing and then moved to Worcester. He seemed to enjoy his time there, taking part in hockey and football coaching and being involved with the Officers' Training Corps. But like many of his contemporaries he was worried about the political situation in Europe, which seemed to be heading towards war.

One of the international initiatives to try to avoid that was to create a Permanent Court of Arbitration which would provide a peaceful means of settling international disputes. There was also a growing peace movement with activists giving their time and skills to support peace projects. The Permanent Court of Arbitration was to be housed in the Peace Palace at The Hague, which was then being built with money provided by Andrew Carnegie, the Scottish-American industrialist.

Oakley left Worcester at the end of the summer term 1912 to work on the Peace Palace. The structure of the building was by then complete and he worked on the interior decorations. Herman Rosse, the Dutch designer and architect who was responsible for most of the interior design, had been a contemporary of Oakley's at the RCA and it may have been that connection which led Oakley to join the project.

The Peace Palace in The Hague. (©The Peace Palace, The Hague (PP))

In his drawing opposite, Oakley shows himself on the staging working on the design of a decorated tile panel of the Peace Palace and its grounds.

The tiled panel showing a plan of the Palace, on which Oakley worked. (PP)

The panel is in the corridor that runs along the back of the Palace. The silhouette portrait at the top is of Andrew Carnegie. The Peace Palace is now the home of the International Court of Justice.

Oakley (top left) working on the decorations of the Peace Palace, The Hague. The dove of peace is posing as the German imperial eagle (as on page 153). (JR)

Exhibition in York, 1913. (JR)

A Small Exhibition of

ORIGINAL SILHOUETTES

By H. LAWRENCE OAKLEY. A.R.C.A. (Lond.)

will be on view on

Thursday, Friday & Saturday, April 24.26

at the Assembly Rooms, York,

from 11 to 6 p.m.

The Silhouettes which consist of Hunting Incidents and scenes from Country Life are cut direct with scissors from paper without any previous sketching.

When Oakley returned to England at Easter 1913 he put on an exhibition of his work in the Assembly Rooms in York. The silhouettes sold well and it was enough to make him decide to see if he could make a living as a silhouettist.

Joyce, Margery (Biddy) and Nesta Smith, 1913. (JR)

The girls were the daughters of Lawrence Oakley's sister Margaret and her husband, Frank Smith. Joyce Smith was the author's mother.

Studio advertisement for Scarborough. (Sally Courage)

In the summer of 1913 Oakley took studios in Harrogate and Scarborough and then went on to the Army & Navy Stores in London for the winter season.

Unknown lady and gentleman taken at the Army & Navy Stores in London, winter 1913–14. (HLOC/ME)

Three of eight carriage posters for the Metropolitan and District Railway Company, 1914. (HLOC/ME)

While Oakley was working in the Army & Navy Stores he was approached by the Metropolitan and District Railway Company to do a series of eight carriage panel posters. The idea was to encourage commuters to use the line for recreational journeys. Though Southend was well beyond the end of the District line there was a through service. Passengers could board a designated Southend train anywhere along the District line and would be taken to Barking, where the engine was changed and the carriages taken on to Southend.

Portrait Group at Perranuthoe, Witsun, 1914. From left to right: H.L. Oakley, Stanley Smith, Acton Pile, Lionel Gwyn and George Denham. (HLOC/ME)

In 1914 Oakley decided to repeat the pattern of the previous year by taking studios at Harrogate and Scarborough, but before that he took a week's holiday in Perranunthoe, Cornwall, with a group of artist friends.

Oakley in his studio at Scarborough, 1914. (HLOC/ME)

Reverend William Almack, Vicar of Ospringe, 1914; Lady in Riding Habit, 1913. (HLOC/ME)

The vicar is in the centre of the second window from the left in Oakley's studio. The lady is on the left edge of the central arched window.

'The Morning Dip, July 1914'. Oakley is sitting second from the left at Scarborough on the eve of war. (HLOC/ME)

When Britain entered the First World War in August 1914, Oakley decided to enlist, as did two of his brothers. He left a note in the window of his studio in Scarborough 'Off to silhouette the Kaiser', with the small figure of a soldier carrying a German helmet on his rifle. The figure shown here is from one of his later pieces, which seems to show the same spirit. (© ILN/Mary Evans Picture Library (ILN/ME))

Chapter 2

Recruiting Posters and Training in England

'A Cheery Farewell'. (HLOC/ME)

'Goodbye, Sir, and when you do go to the front I shall look in the Casualty List for your name every day.'

York station, January 1915. (HLOC/ME)

While Oakley was waiting to start his training he designed a recruiting poster, which was sent to the Parliamentary Recruiting Committee in London by a contact in the North Eastern Railway Company in York. The big railway companies were pioneers in advertising and their support would carry considerable weight. It will have helped, too, that the Deputy General Manager of the NER, Eric Geddes, was on the Committee. The design was accepted and he was paid 5 guineas for it.

Geddes had greatly improved the efficiency of the NER and was one of the outstanding figures in the railway industry. With the support of the Prime Minister, Lloyd George, he was later made Director General of Transportation in France with the honorary rank of Major General. The improvements he made to the railway system enabled troops and supplies to be delivered to the front much more quickly and were an important factor in improving the British performance in the field.

The 'Think' poster was also used in Australia and the image was used with different wording in Canada.

After the reorganisation of the railways in Britain in 1923, the London and North Eastern Railway became one of Oakley's biggest commercial customers.

The 'Think' poster as used in Britain. Oakley's figure of the advancing soldier became one of the most recognisable images of the war. (Imperial War Museum (IWM))

The Australian version, with clearer lettering. (IWM)

(IWM)

Canadian posters using Oakley's image. (IWM)

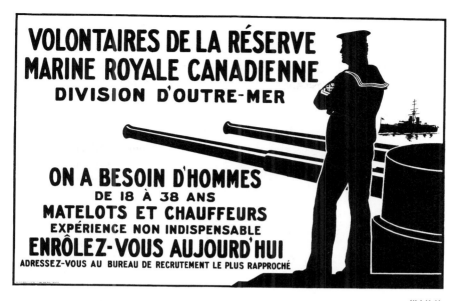

The success of his 'Think' poster led to a commission from the Admiralty for a poster for the Royal Navy. He was given two days to produce a design and paid 10 guineas. His design was again used in Canada, in English and French language versions. He had not signed the 'Think' poster but he did sign this one. Together the two posters made his name and opened the way for him to have his work published throughout the war.

Oakley, sitting on the ground third from the left, with his intake at
Woodcote barracks. (Margaret Rowe (MR))

In November 1914, Oakley started his initial training with the 21st
Battalion of the Royal Fusiliers at Woodcote Park barracks near Epsom. He
wrote to an aunt on New Year's Day to tell her about his Christmas Day:

On Xmas Day I was acting corporal to the Medical Officer and had to light
his fire at 7.30 and enter the names and complaints of about 50 sick men
while he examined them. Our duties were over by 9 am so as I was excused
from Church Parade I went back to breakfast and on to the church near us
on my own. Our Christmas dinner was not a very great affair, we had some
rather dry beef a plum pudding and some mince pies, but Houghton had a
box of good things so we finished up with dates apples figs cake, chocolates
and crackers.

I spent Xmas afternoon patching the seat of one pair of trousers with the
remains of another so could not go to dine with the Spencers. I have now got
my uniform in toto so am clothed again.

Sergeant Major R.B. Bull of the Royal Fusiliers: 'The man who puts us through it.' (MR)

At the end of his course in May 1915 Oakley was commissioned as a Second Lieutenant in the Yorkshire Regiment, the Green Howards. The name Green Howards goes back to a time when regiments took the name of their Colonel and two regiments, each with a Colonel Howard, happened to be brigaded together. The colours of the flashes on their uniforms, green and buff, were used to distinguish between them. The name was informal until 1920 when it became part of the full name of the Yorkshire Regiment.

After several further reviews and mergers, the position until recently was that each of the three regular battalions of the Yorkshire Regiment carried the name of one of the historic regiments: 1st Battalion (The Princess of Wales' Own); 2nd Battalion (The Green Howards); and the 3rd Battalion (The Duke of Wellington's). Following another review in 2012 the number of regular battalions was reduced to two. They carry no historic names but the traditions and values of the Green Howards now live on in the whole of the Yorkshire Regiment, alongside those of the other antecedent regiments.

Like most soldiers Oakley's first loyalty was to his regiment and he remained 'of the 8th Yorkshire Regiment, the Green Howards' for the rest of his life and on his headstone. But for much of his army career he held

Major General Sir J.M. Babington GOC of the 23rd Division. (HLOC/ME)

posts in the headquarters of the 69th Brigade, of which the 8th Yorkshires were a part, and later at divisional level. This gave him a wider range of experience and a broader perspective than most junior officers.

With two other newly commissioned officers from his initial training course Oakley joined the 8th Green Howards at West Hartlepool in May 1915. The battalion had already been in training for several months and Oakley and his Woodcote colleagues had missed some of the essential parts of the platoon commander's course. So when the 8th Yorkshires and the 69th Brigade went to France in August, they had to stay behind to finish the course.

The 69th Brigade fought as part of the 23rd Infantry Division under the command of Major General Sir J.M. Babington. He was known to his men as 'Babs' but was nonetheless highly regarded by them, as well as by the high command. He made the 23rd into one of the most effective new army divisions and stayed with them almost to the end of the war, when he was promoted to Lieutenant General and given command of an army corps.

Before their departure to join the British Expeditionary Force in France the Division was inspected by King George V accompanied by Queen Mary. The King's message began, 'You are about to join your comrades at the Front in bringing to a successful end this relentless War of over twelve months' duration', reflecting the prevailing view that the war would soon be over.

At the time of embarkation the infantry units in the 23rd Division were:

68th Infantry Brigade: 10th and 11th Northumberland Fusiliers, 12th and 13th Durham Light Infantry.

69th Infantry Brigade: 11th West Yorkshire Regiment, 8th and 9th Yorkshire Regiment, 10th Duke of Wellington's Regiment.

70th Infantry Brigade: 11th Sherwood Foresters, 8th King's Own Yorkshire Light Infantry, 8th and 9th York and Lancaster Regiment.

Together with their pioneer, artillery, engineering and other service components there would have been 12,000–15,000 men.

There would also have been a very large number of horses, certainly many hundreds and possibly into the thousands. Although the 23rd was not a mounted infantry division, horses were the main trasport for officers and supplies. There would also have been a lot of mules, which were more suited to pulling limbers across country. Not all the animals would have travelled on the first crossing, however.

Lawrence Oakley (standing centre) with his family, September 1915. (JR)

The family had gathered for the funeral of Lawrence's aunt, Miss Emma Oakley, at her home in Buttington, near Welshpool. It was the only time during the war that the family was together. Oakley's mother is on the left.

Richard (sitting centre) was in the Denbighshire Hussars but later transferred to the Machine Gun Corps. He was seriously injured at the Battle of Passchendaele in an action for which he won the Military Cross and was then invalided out of the Army. Jack (standing right) was also in the Denbighshire Hussars. He was an art teacher and a talented silhouettist. The eldest brother, Alan, in civilian clothes, was an engineer and served later in the Royal Engineers Reserves.

Their sister Margaret (right) was married to Frank Smith, a bank manager for the York City and County bank. She was the author's grandmother.

A few days after the funeral, Lawrence Oakley crossed to France to join his colleagues.

Chapter 3

Armentières and the Somme

The ruined church at Bois Grenier, December 1915. (JR)

A dug-out in reserve trenches at Armentières. (JR)

The 23rd Division crossed from Southampton to Boulogne and according to Lieutenant Colonel H.R. Sandilands' book, *The 23rd Division 1914–1919*, the crossing went perfectly except for some trouble with the conscripts – the horses. Some had refused to pull baggage wagons and one jumped into the dock on arrival at Bolougne. After a period of further training, the Division moved into reserve trenches on a quiet sector of the front near Armentières.

The trenches they had taken over from the French were shallow and poorly constructed. They kept the parapet in good repair, as Oakley shows here, but they had not started to deepen and strengthen the trenches because they expected to be moving on soon. The Division had been put on notice to be ready to move forward on its front during the Battle of Loos. The Division was not in the order of battle, but the intention was that by moving forward it would tie in the Germans on its sector, so that they could not be moved to help to deal with the anticipated British breakthrough at Loos. But there was no breakthrough and the Division had to dig in where it was for a long stay.

'What to do with Our Surplus War Posters', *The Bystander*,
8 September 1915. (ILN/ME)

This cartoon, by Alick Ritchie, includes both of Oakley's posters (top left and bottom right). It reflected the assumption, still widely held in Britain, that the war would end soon. That was particularly ironic in light of the heavy defeat later that month at Loos.

A TOKEN OF SYMPATHY
FROM OUR TOMMIES

(MR)

Oakley joined his unit in early October and wrote home with his first impressions. The troops had made a memorial garden where a French child had been killed and the 8th Yorkshires had also suffered several casualties from shellfire. And there had been a fight between two fellow officers:

> Unfortunately Larner and Watson who hate each other had a terrific fight in a field on the way and Watson who is the nicer fellow came off badly and his face on arrival here was a picture, all swollen his nose cut and covered in iodine. The C.O. asked him if he had had an accident on the way.

He knew that he was not allowed to mention place names in a letter, but he got the message across nonetheless: 'I am not allowed to say where I am but watch the initials and you won't be far wrong. Are many enlisting now? The inhabitants 'ere realise etc.'

One of the duties of a junior officer was to supervise the rum ration. (JR)

H.L.O. in reserve trenches. Bois Grenier
Church in background. (JR)

La-Noulette Church. (JR)

H.L.O. on the duckboards. (JR)

In the mess at Moat Farm, later blown
to bits. (JR)

Captain Dodgson (killed), H.L.O. and
Lieutenant Hume-Wright (killed). (JR)

Captain F. Dodgson and Second Lieutenant Hume-Wright, both of
the 8th Yorkshires, were killed during the capture of Contalmaison on
10 July 1916.

'Going on leave'.   'Returning'.

'An Officer of the 8th Yorks is reported to have returned one night from Patrol with a Bicycle taken from a German Trench.' Our Artist was not present but, like the 'Daily Mirror', depicts the scene as it appears to his imagination. Parapet marked with an X.

The Dump, Christmas 1915. (HLOC/ME)

Each Christmas between 1915 and 1918 the 23rd Division produced a magazine called *The Dump*. Its format was much the same as any house magazine, with humorous articles, poems, drawings and cartoons. Oakley contributed this page and the one opposite.

Further fields for padres at the front. No. 1: 'Reading to a Working Party'.

Further fields for padres at the front. No. 2: 'A Pied Padre charming away Rats from the Trenches'.

(HLOC/ME)

The tone of the magazine was unfailingly one of wry humour and stoical optimism. It also managed to attract high-quality contributions, most from within the Division but some from guest contributors, including established names from the arts and entertainment worlds.

Lawrence Oakley taking the portrait of a fellow officer. (HLOC/ME)

Oakley took hundreds of portraits during the war. He didn't charge for them and they made good mementos to send home. This self-portrait was done after the war for an article in a children's magazine.

After the Battle of Loos there were no further major engagements for the rest of the autumn and winter. The 23rd Division remained in the Armentières area until they were moved to the Souchez front in March, when preparations were beginning for the spring campaign.

During the winter lull, the Division carried out a number of raids on German trenches: a practice which both armies started to do at this stage of the war. Raids would involve a small number of troops, up to about company strength of around 100 men, and were carried out at night. As well as killing Germans the objectives might include taking prisoners – for intelligence purposes – gathering information and destroying particular installations.

Although the front line was static, there was a constant movement of units and men between the front line, the reserve trenches and the rear. In a letter to his brother Jack, of 19 December 1915, Oakley gave this account of his movements:

We have been in luck lately 4 days in awful muddy front line 4 days in reserve billets and 4 days in support instead of front line and then 8 days in 'rest' billets. Tonight however I have to take my platoon into some supports nearer the firing line and stay awake all night to be ready in case of an attack.

The top of the cover of *The Bystander*, 8 March 1916. (ILN/ME)

The Bystander first published Oakley's silhouettes on 8 March 1916, introducing his column with the masthead 'Trench Life in Silhouette' on the cover of the magazine. He was in good company. Bruce Bairnsfather was one of a very talented group of illustrators and cartoonists at the magazine, which also included H.M. Bateman and W. Heath Robinson. Oakley produced material for them for the rest of the war and for several years afterwards, and was sometimes known as 'Oakley of the Bystander'. But he was never on the staff.

Though Oakley's silhouettes were published under the general heading 'Trench Life in Silhouette' he did not attempt to convey the carnage and extreme suffering which so characterise the First World War. Instead he used dry humour and shrewd observation to show how soldiers and local people coped with life under such conditions. All magazines were censored but there are no signs that Oakley felt unduly restricted by that. He wouldn't have wanted to show the terrible things he saw. He was in tune with the ethos of the times; when circumstances were bad you focused on how you survived in spite of them, not on how awful they were. There was no hatred towards the Germans; he poked fun at them but no more than at local people or indeed the British themselves.

The Bystander thrived during the First World War and remained independent until 1940 when it merged with *The Tatler*.

TRENCH LIFE

A WORKING PARTY

THE IDEAL

AFTERNOON TEA

FIRST-HAND IMPRESSIONS, VISUALISED ON THE SPOT,

IN SILHOUETTE

A LISTENING POST

THE REAL

A WELCOME WASH

MARCHING UP A COMMUNICATION TRENCH

DAILY (AND NIGHTLY) ROUTINE OF THE FIRING LINE

BY SECOND-LIEUT. H. L. OAKLEY

Oakley's first piece in *The Bystander*, 8 March 1916. (ILN/ME)

A working party, the Armentières sector, early 1916. (MR)

Scenes from behind the front lines in Flanders, *The Bystander*, 12 April 1916. (ILN/ME)

MULE LIMBER BRINGING UP SUPPLIES

A COMMON OBSTRUCTION IN THE WAY OF THE STAFF OFFICER

FRENCH SUPPLY TROOPS LOADING UP THEIR BEER CART

FROM THE TRENCHES TO BILLETS: PASSING A CALVARY

'Night Work in Silhouette', *The Bystander*, 17 May 1916. (ILN/ME)

'There is little traffic in the day–time behind the lines, but at night everybody is suddenly and violently busy. Rations and shells are brought up, and the heavy motor lorries claim right of way from everything and everybody else.'

"BRODIE" PATTERN STEEL HELMET
(War Office Pattern) in use.

" My Platoon was holding the Trench round the Crater at the time, and Captain Richardson was going round in the morning visiting the sentries ; as I came up the Trench Captain Richardson was just picking up his helmet and he told me he thought someone must have whacked him on the head with a stick. I heard the shot, and the sentry had just warned the Captain that a sniper was busy. The force of the bullet knocked the helmet off and made the Captain jump off the step. If it had not been for the helmet I am certain we should have lost our O.C. Company."

German Lines

Crater

Chord Line

PLAN showing position of Capt. R. and where shot came from.

H. L. OAKLEY, 2nd-Lieut.,
8th Battalion Yorkshire Regiment.
19th May, 1916.

(MR)

The original Brodie steel helmet was introduced in late 1915, and there were only enough for use on the front line. When a unit was relieved the helmets were left for the new unit. By the summer of 1916 there were enough helmets of an improved design for all troops to have them. Oakley's advertisement was aimed at junior officers, some of whom may have been reluctant to wear them. Commanders had presumably decided to use persuasion as well as orders. The main benefit of a helmet was to give protection against shrapnel injuries but deflecting a sniper's bullet may have been a more persuasive image for junior officers.

The German army made a similar change, introducing the *Stahlhelm* to replace the much loved *Pickelhaube* helmet, though senior officers continued to wear it on ceremonial occasions. A *Pickelhaube* was a highly prized trophy. Oakley's mother wanted one but he could only get her a steel helmet.

AN OFFICER'S DUG-OUT

A YOUNG SUB

THE STAFF

OH! I SAY!

Lieut. H. L. Oakley produces by means of his silhouettes, cut directly with scissors from paper, a freshness and directness of e which the artist who uses pen or brush cannot obtain. He has from his nursery days been a keen silhouettist; and his knowl of drawing and power of observation have, through years of practice, dowered him with the sure and confident touch whi

RATIONS

AN ARCADIAN TOUCH

CLEANING RIFLES

A HEATED ARGUMENT

SENTRIES

A PATROL

DIXIE-LAND ("DIXIE" IS THE NAME GIVEN TO TOMMY'S COOKING POT)

BY SECOND-LIEUT. H. L. OAKLEY

coping-stone of his art. Lieut. Oakley, after being in the Public Schools Corps at Epsom early in the war, received a Commission and now been at the Front for seven months. When serving as a private he executed the well-known war posters. "Think!" and "Remember!" houette figures of a soldier and a sailor, respectively, the first for the Army, the second for the Navy Recruiting Committee

'Staff, Subs, Sentries & Surprises Silhouetted', *The Bystander*, 24 May 1916. (ILN/ME)

'How our soldiers are made; incidents in training of Our New Armies',
The Bystander, 21 June 1916. (ILN/ME)

At the planning stages for the Battle of the Somme, which started ten days after this was published, it was intended to be 'the Big Push'. Haig's vision was that the artillery would smash the first line of the defences, the infantry would push the Germans back, and the cavalry would exploit the breakthrough. The commander, General Rawlinson, was more cautious and there were no cavalry units in the starting order of battle.

'How our Soldiers are Mended', *The Bystander*, 21 June 1916. (ILN/ME)

This was a companion piece to the one opposite. Oakley was sent back to England on sick leave in May and it draws from his own experiences. He crossed the Channel on the SS *St George*.

Lieutenant Donald Bell VC of the 9th Yorkshire Regiment. (The Green Howards Museum)

Oakley missed most of the Battle of the Somme because he was in England on sick leave. But his regiment, the Green Howards, was heavily involved. Its most notable contribution was in the capture of the village of Contalmaison.

The village had been attacked by the 34th Division on the opening day of the battle, 1 July, and a small group of Royal Scots fought their way into the village. But there was not enough support to enable them to hold on, and according to one account they were 'wiped out'. There is now a memorial to them near the village church.

The 23rd Division relieved the 34th when the attack was resumed on 7 July. This time, the 1st Worcesters entered the village but prolonged heavy rain brought the attack to a standstill and German artillery fire drove them out.

Finally, on 10 July, after a bayonet charge to take the first German line, the village was retaken by the 8th and 9th Green Howards, plus two companies from the 11th West Yorkshires. They took more than 250 prisoners and captured several machine guns, which they turned on the fleeing Germans and used again later to hold off a German counter-attack.

During the main attack, Lieutenant Donald Bell of the 9th Green Howards won the VC for leading two men to capture a machine-gun post. Before the war he had been a professional footballer with Bradford Park Avenue. He was killed a few days later fighting off another German counter-attack. His medals including the VC were purchased by the Professional Footballer's Association in 2010 for a reported price of more than £200,000.

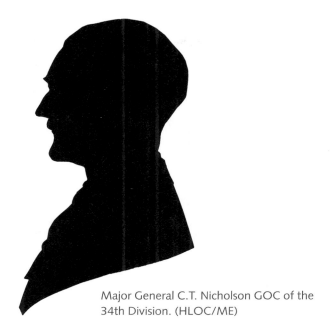

Major General C.T. Nicholson GOC of the 34th Division. (HLOC/ME)

Major General Nicholson took command of the 34th Division after his predecessor had been killed by artillery fire near Contalmaison.

(JR)

Lochnager crater between La Boisselle and Contalmaison was the largest of the many craters created by mines exploded under German positions on the first day of the Battle of the Somme. The coach parked on the edge gives an idea of its size.

'Soldiers, Sailors, School-boys, Sisters, all in Silhouette', *The Bystander*, 16 August 1916. (ILN/ME)

During a fortnight in the trenches in April, Oakley contracted severe diarrhoea (then usually described as dysentry) and was sent to the Red Cross hospital in Rouen, where he cut these impressions. He said of the two dogs: 'The English terrier turns up his nose at the curiously harnessed French dog.'

Sketches made in the Red Cross hospital in Rouen, 1916. (MR)

(MR)

From Rouen, Oakley was sent back to England to the military hospital at
Rugeley in Staffordshire. He then had six weeks of convalescence and was
passed fit for light duties and posted to the training depot of the 11th Yorkshire
Regiment, also at Rugeley.

'Proverbs from the Push in Silhouette', *The Bystander*, 13 September 1916. (ILN/ME)

This somewhat whimsical piece of reflections after the Battle of the Somme was done while Oakley was still with the 11th Yorkshires in England. He had been passed fit for general service by a medical board at the end of May and wanted to return to France but the platoon he was training was partway through its course and the 11th Yorkshires kept him on until it finished.

'A platoon I trained at Rugeley in 1916 from their first day to the day they went out on a draft to France'. (MR)

(MR)

Portraits of Major Carey (left) and Brigadier General Leach (right) at Rugeley, with the 11th Yorkshire Regiment at Rugeley barracks in Staffordshire.

'Proverbs for the "Pushful"', *The Bystander*, 31 January 1917. (ILN/ME)

This page was intended to be a companion piece to the 'Proverbs from the Push in Silhouette' on page 64, but it was held up by the censor and was not published until January.

Both useful and ornamental

Flying Men

Old stagers of the New Army

The Staff

Padre and "Sister"

Reinforcements

Escorting

H·L·OAKLEY

'The Silhouettist on Shipboard'; 'Going Out', *The Bystander*, 2 May 1917. (ILN/ME)

The 11th Yorkshires released Oakley in January 1917, and he travelled back to France to rejoin the 8th Battalion.

Chapter 4

Messines and the Ypres Salient

Anything to report? (MR)

'The Stunt of the Billeting Officer', *The Bystander*, 25 April 1917. (ILN/ME)

In March 1917, the 23rd Division moved from the Armentières sector towards the Ypres Salient to prepare for the next campaign. Oakley was the billeting officer for the 8th Yorkshires. At about the same time he took on the job of Assistant Adjutant, which he said the CO had offered him to make it easier for his bald head and old age.

The Horse Lines

A Field Forge

The Transport Officer

The "Heavies"—An Agricultural Touch

The "Q.-M."

Limbers Ready to Go Up to the Line

THE TRANSPORT LINES

Lieut. Oakley shows us in silhouette some aspects of the Infantry Transport, which is the connecting link between the men in the trenches and the Supply Column. Although the lines are at a safe distance from the front, the transport enters the danger zone every evening when taking up supplies to the "Dump" behind the trenches

'"Supply" Silhouetted', *The Bystander*, 11 April 1917. (ILN/ME)

German guns dominated the Ypres Salient so supplies could only be moved at night.

Captain Delayne, the Quartermaster of the 8th Yorkshire Regiment, appears in several of Oakley's pieces including the one opposite. (MR)

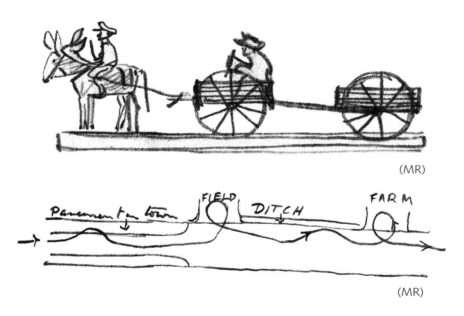

(MR)

(MR)

Oakley told his mother of his own recent trip on a mule limber. The mules were so stubborn that the only way to get them past a field opening or farm entrance was for the driver to dismount and lead them into the opening, make a circle and come out. They would not walk on the right-hand side of the road, and the limber damaged two vehicles and forced several others into the ditch.

'Spring in Silhouette', *The Bystander*, 16 May 1917. (ILN/ME)

In the war zone, spring meant the start of a new season of battles.

Aerial photograph of the German trench system near Hill 60, showing the ground pitted with shell-holes and several craters from earlier mine explosions. (IWM)

The main British objective for the summer of 1917 was to break out of the Ypres Salient and push for the channel ports, but before doing that, they had to drive the Germans from the Messines Ridge that overlooked the city. The 8th Yorkshires were given the key task of attacking the two main heights on the ridge, Hill 60 and the Caterpillar, which stood on either side of a deep railway cutting. In preparation for the attack, Oakley made a model of the local terrain and the German trenches. This is the account from Lt-Col H.R. Sandilands' book *The 23rd Division 1914–1919*:

> Lt. H.L Oakley of the 8th Yorkshire Regiment, celebrated as an artist for his exquisite silhouettes, constructed a model of the Caterpillar and Hill 60 from maps and air photographs, showing the hostile trenches, railway, and the general detail of the ground. Study of this proved of immense value to officers and N.C.Os who before the attack felt they knew the German trench system as well as their own.

The first phase of the battle was a massive artillery barrage lasting almost three weeks. When the barrage stopped just before 3 a.m. on 7 June the Germans anticipated an attack and manned their defensives. The British then detonated a million pounds of explosives in tunnels under the German positions and it was said that Lloyd George heard the noise in London. The 8th Yorkshires reached the top of Hill 60 within an hour and the whole ridge was cleared in a week. It was the most complete British victory of the war so far and the first battle in which the defenders suffered more casualties than the attackers: estimated at 25,000 German and 17,000 British.

Photograph taken from a German soldier captured at Messines. (JR)

Officers of the 69th Brigade with material captured at Messines. Brigadier General Lambert is sitting front centre holding his cap; Oakley is standing back right wearing his cap. (JR)

In the Battle Field (Literally).

Dear Mater 12.6.17.

You will see by the paper we have had a show which has been very successful indeed Our Brigade & particularly our Battalion covered itself with glory

12th June 1917

Dear Mater,

You will see by the paper we have had a show which has been very successful indeed. Our Brigade and particularly our Battalion covered itself with glory. As Assistant Adjutant I was left out of the stunt in charge of 100 odd men for reinforcements. I was the only one out except two on leave and one on a course. I suppose I am lucky. I am glad to say the Colonel is safe and the Adjutant also but two of my Company's officers were killed including Capt. Lambert who was with me at Hartlepool. I have the sad task of notifying their people. Tolson has a very nasty wound in the arm again. It has been an anxious time for us all, so much so that I could not keep out of it altogether but went up two nights after the attack to see them hanging on in the trenches we had taken.

Our men had the task of taking the famous place (Hill 60) after the largest mine that has ever been blown. I had the pleasure of going over the top and in the huge crater and down the further side where so many have lost their lives these last 2 years and 6 months.

It was a grand sight at 3.10 a.m. to see the mines blow up; and the barrage of our guns was the most awful yet. Our troops were so splendid that they got on too fast for the barrage and many were wounded and killed this way. The poor Bosches would do nothing but 'Kamarade' and by 9 a.m. prisoners were passing thro' the camp in the back area. We got a lot of loot out of the dug-outs etc; but no one knows how many poor devils of theirs were buried by the mines. Miller was in charge of a Company but the day before he was taken ill and went to Hospital with Mumps of all things. He positively cried poor beggar as he was the keenest officer we have, and would certainly have won honours.

I slept in a field last night under a bush through the most intense noise of our guns - one battery being 100 yards away. The Bosch replied occasionally and we felt a bit windy at times. A poor Devil has just been wounded in the field and has gone down to the Dressing station. I am Adjutant again now as Bush has gone on leave. I hope to get mine within another month if all goes well. I have been working very hard lately and have made a model of the country including the Hill and railway cutting. The C.O. is very pleased and also the General but we have not got the best material to make the show a success. I can't tell you much but there was no hitch as far as we were concerned and the casualties are mostly wounded and light compared with other attacks.

Love to Aunty and self.

Yours, Lawrence.

Oakley's letter to his mother about the Battle of Messines.

'Women Workers in the War Zone', *The Bystander*, 4 July 1917. (ILN/ME)

Oakley got the leave he was hoping for and cut this piece in England. He said that he had actually witnessed all of these scenes in Flanders and added that women did *all* of the work in the absence of the men. He has re-created the scenes as an allegorical picture about women's equality. The figures are everywoman, not just Flemish peasants.

'The Tide of Victory', *The Bystander*, 8 August 1917. (ILN/ME)

The decisive victory at Messines created the expectation that the tide would carry forward into the Third Battle of Ypres (Passchendaele). But by the time this piece was published, a week into the battle, it was becoming clear that the momentum had not been sustained. Oakley's brother Richard was severely wounded and won an MC in the battle.

'On leave in the town', *The Bystander*, 5 September 1917. (ILN/ME)

Oakley shows his pride and pleasure at being a soldier on leave in London.

'On leave in the country', *The Bystander*, 5 September 1917. (ILN/ME)

In the country, informality and elegant leisure were the order of the day.

Lt H.L. Oakley by Jens Handrup, London 1917. (HLOC/ME)

While Oakley was in London he had his portrait taken by Jens Handrup, the Danish silhouettist who worked in London during the early decades of the twentieth century. He had studios in D.H. Evans in Oxford Street and at the Crystal Palace, and was unusual in cutting three thicknesses of paper. He was killed in a traffic accident in Oxford Street in 1931.

'Subaltern Stunts'. (ILN/ME)

Before Oakley could return to his unit he was taken ill again and didn't go back to Flanders until October. His medical record for this period is blank but if his treatment followed the pattern of his last illness he would have spent time in hospital followed by convalescence and then light duties with a unit in England. Skindle's Hotel and Restaurant on the Thames at Maidenhead was a popular rendezvous with army officers.

A well-known war correspondent writing a description of English troops in action

A sergeant-major refusing the surplus rum

An old soldier missing the leave train

R.T.O.: "Yes, it's up to time to-day, but you may catch it if you like to run!"

PASSED BY CENSOR

A chaplain reading to a working party

'Things I Have Never Seen at the Front', *The Bystander*, 3 October 1917. (ILN/ME)

The piece at the top left was aimed at W. Beach Thomas of the *Daily Mail*, who Oakley thought gave disproportionate coverage to actions by Scottish and Dominion troops. But in Australia, Canada and New Zealand there were strong feelings that actions by their troops were too often described simply as involving British troops.

Caricatures of a number of wounded officers by Lieutenant Fred May, *The Tatler*,
12 December 1917. (ILN/ME)

Fred May spent several months at Fovant military hospital in Hampshire in 1917 so these caricatures were probably taken there. By the time this was published Oakley had returned to his unit and was serving in Italy.

'The Strafes of the Subaltern in Silhouette' from a special WHY-NOT? edition of
The Bystander, 10 October 1917. (ILN/ME)

Chapter 5

Italy

Villerverla, south of the Assiago plateau. (MR)

An Italian Gig (ILN/ME)

Soon after Oakley returned to Flanders in November 1917, he was on the move again, this time to Italy. The Austrian Army, reinforced by several German divisions, had broken the Italian line at Caporetto and four French and six British divisions, including the 23rd, were sent to help the Italians.

It was an extraordinary change for the British troops. They had experienced the hardships and dangers of war on the battlefields of northern France and the devastation of the Ypres Salient. Now they travelled by train through Paris, down the Rhone valley to the south of France and on across the Riviera into Italy where they were welcomed as heroes.

Oakley wrote to his mother on 15 November shortly after they arrived:

Just a line to say that I am fit and very well and enjoying life A1. We had a tremendous reception en route. I was sorry we passed most of the Riviera in the dark but I got out at Cannes and thought of you and Aunt J. At Genoa we had a semi public reception and the station was placarded 'WELCOME to our verry brave English … etc.' Italian ladies gave us wine and favours and our own band played lively tunes and the Italian national anthem.

We were 4 days and 5 nights in the train and marched here (Rivalta sul Mincio) about 10 miles after. Through Mantova we had flowers thrown from the windows and people wore chrysanthemums and coloured ribbons. We were the first English in this village and of course the boys are having the time of their lives. The weather is mild and sunny, we are miles from the front and all is merry and bright. Have plenty of togs and food, grapes and apples galore. The girls are very pretty and the kids are all over me.

(MR)

'Silhouettes from the Sunny South', *The Bystander*, 18 January 1918. (ILN/ME)

'After the long railway journey we are billeted in a small village (Rivalta) for a few days to get acclimatised and ready for the long march to the field of operations.'

After a few days of rest the 23rd Division marched 120 miles to the front at Montello, a hill overlooking the Piave River near Treviso. Oakley was the billeting officer for the 8th Yorkshire Regiment and he explained his duties in a letter to his uncle:

I go ahead with 4 sergeants on bicycles, start about 6am and arrive in the village allocated to us at about 8.30. We then chalk up the billets and interview the inhabitants. I have to provide barns or empty rooms for 1,000 men, accommodation for 54 horses and waggons, beds where possible for 36 officers, a store for the baggage waggons to unload, an aid post and an orderly room. And all the time the battalion is marching on our heels and very tired when they arrive, and if one has not been successful one gets a thin time.

One place we were all in an empty furnished palace with sheets etc., a magnificent house equipped with furniture and pictures. Other times like the present we mess in a kitchen with a wood fire and the family eat in the same room. A platoon of men sleep in the hay loft and the field kitchen is in the fold yard. We have killed a fatted goose today and live well on eggs and fresh butter. We are able to buy flour for the men and some fresh vegetables. This is a hundred times better than the BONEYARD [Ypres Salient].

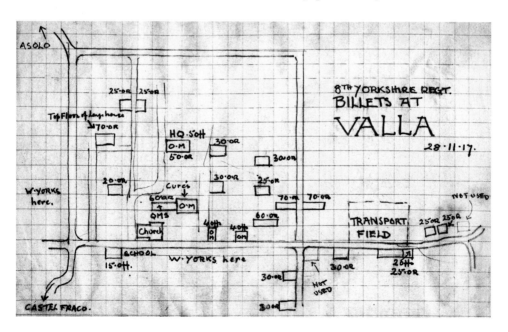

Billeting plan for the night of 28 November 1917 for the village of Valla near Castelfranco. OR is other ranks. OM is officers' mess. (MR)

The Italians had stabilised the front on the Piave River before the British reached the line, so the 23rd Division was able to take up its position on the Montello without having to go straight into battle. Their headquarters were in the nearby town of Montebelluna.

In the six months during which Oakley was in Italy there were no major battles. There were skirmishes, raids and occasional shelling but compared with Flanders it was a holiday.

The high spirits of the troops were reflected in the review and pantomime that the Division put on at Christmas. One of the songs went:

> *I'm Monty from Montebelluna, the bounder from far Biadene,*
> *I'm a hell of a fellow around the Montello,*
> *The road-hog of Road 17.*
> *I'm Prince of the river Piave, the pride of my bally platoon,*
> *And the girls of Padova all sigh and turn over*
> *For Monty of Montebelluna.*

After a few weeks on the Montello the division marched about 50 miles west to the Asiago plateau (altopiano) where they spent most of their time in Italy.

FARA. March 1918.

Fara Vincentino on the edge of the Asiago plateau. 'I was area commandant for a fortnight at Fara.' (MR)

THE ALTOPIANO

The girls of the ALTOPIANO
Are as sweet as the ones in MILANO,
There's a dear little peach
Lives on MONTE LINTECHE,
Who's decidedly far from 'piano'.

There was a fair maide of LEMERLE,
Whose hair was both silky and curly,
And she lived up a spout
Near the OXFORD REDOUBT,
Where the crumps made her hair a bit whirly.

'SILVIA'

(MR)

Another young fairy from CODA,
Knew nothing of love, till Jack showed her,
Then she'd hug and she'd kiss
Through the long nights of bliss
In the GHELPAC Canoe – whilst he rowed her.

Still another wee puss at CESUNA,
Found a handsome young soldier to spoon her,
When he asked her to wed
She just simpered, and said,
'You're too slow – Sergeant Smith asked me sooner.'

THERESINA

ANGELINA

Oakley later wrote a poem in limerick style about the girls of the altopiano. (JR)

'The Spirit of Christmas', *The Bystander Annual*, 1917. (ILN/ME)

Oakley is making a point about the constancy of the spirit of Christmas. The 'Avante' and 'Apres' characters and settings are the same. During the war the characters are in uniform and the setting is different but the spirit is the same.

Brig.-Gen. Lambert, GOC 69th Brigade and
Maj.-Gen. Babington, GOC 23rd Division.

[Extract from Warrant Officer's Letter]
Please note that this officer's
movements are entirely governed by
the exigencies of the Service.

Three of Oakley's pieces in *The Dump*, Christmas 1917. (JR)

The back cover of *The Dump*, Christmas 1917. (JR)

The soldier is Private Dale of the 8th Yorkshire Regiment.

ON THE WAY UP COUNTRY

IN A FARM KITCHEN

THE ARRIVAL OF THE COOKER

The march from the Montello to the Asiago plateau, *The Bystander*,
6 March 1918. (ILN/ME)

The priest could not be persuaded to join his guests for dinner because it was a fast day. 'The travelling kitchens were objects of great interest to the Italian women, and the "feathered" legs of the "heavies" a source of delight and wonder.'

95

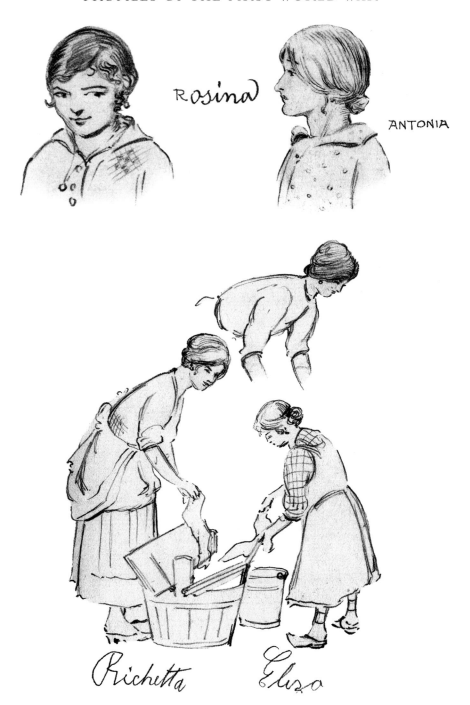

'The girls are very pretty'. *(MR)*

'Snips from the City (Padova) in Silhouette', *The Bystander*, 15 March 1918. (ILN/ME)

'These scenes show a Mess President purchasing necessaries – and a few luxuries. He meets many types of allied troops and his luckier brethren from corps and G.H.Q.'

GUIDES, POSTCARDS, AND SOUVENIRS

"REGIONS" CÆSAR NEVER KNEW

THE PAPAL GUARD

"I CAN'T UNDERSTAND WHY PEOPLE STARE SO!"

PASSED BY CENSOR   DO NOT TALK TO THE DRIVER, AS THERE   THE STREETS ARE EVEN MORE DANGEROUS
                         BEING NO TRAFFIC CONTROL,   THAN THE ITALIAN TRENCHES

'Subaltern Stunts', *The Bystander*, 15 May 1918. (ILN/ME)

Scenes taken while Oakley was on leave in Rome and Florence. The 'I can't understand why people stare so' scene is a caricature of Gen. Lambert with Oakley.

VIEWING ANCIENT—AND
MODERN—ROME

TYPES OF ITALIAN
OFFICERS

FIVE O'CLOCK TEA ON THE TERRACE AT "OLD ENGLAND"

'Subaltern Stunts', *The Bystander*, 15 May 1918. (ILN/ME)

Captain J. Tilly MC. (MR)

Captain Tilly died of wounds received on 8 June 1918 when he led a company of the 8th Yorkshires on a raid of the Austrian trenches. Three other members of the company were slightly injured, but four Germans were killed and eleven taken prisoner, so it was regarded as a successful raid.

Captain Tilly was a highly regarded company commander. He had previously distinguished himself during the Battle of the Menin Road, part of the Battle of Paschendaele.

'Scissored Silhouettes in the Land of the Caesars', *The Bystander*, 29 May 1918. (ILN/ME)

There was no story behind this piece. Oakley was simply enjoying the everyday sights of the Italian countryside.

'Women Workers in Italy', *The Bystander*, 3 July 1918. (ILN/ME)

'Tommy, who ever has an eye for beauty, is always ready to give a hand with the work.'

(ILN/ME)

This piece, done several months after Oakley had returned to France, has the same lyrical quality as the piece on women workers opposite. He is imagining scenes based on his fond memories of Italy, not depicting them literally. Thiene is a town on the southern edge of the Asiago plateau.

One of the billets used by the 8th Yorkshires in Italy. (MR)

At the end of May, Brig.-Gen. Lambert was promoted to Major General and given command of the 32nd Division in Flanders. He appointed Oakley as his ADC and they returned to take up their new posts. ADCs are personal appointments and when Oakley left Italy he was transferred from the Green Howards to the 96th (Lancashire) Brigade within the 32nd Division.

The 8th Yorkshires and the 23rd Division remained in Italy. They fought in the Battle of Vittorio Veneto, which ended the war there on 4 November. After the initial breakthrough by Italian and British forces it became known that the Austrian emperor wanted a ceasefire and the fighting spirit in the Austrian Army evaporated. In the last ten days of the war the Italians took more than 400,000 prisoners and it was one of the most decisive victories of the war.

Oakley would have followed the fortunes of the 8th Yorkshires with close interest. His six months in Italy had been a golden period between the extremes of the Ypres Salient and the fierce intensity of the war during the last few months in France.

Chapter 6

Return to Flanders and the Hundred Days Offensive

NEAR RENINGHELST.

A ruined farm building near Reninghelst in Flanders. (Christopher Rolfe (CR))

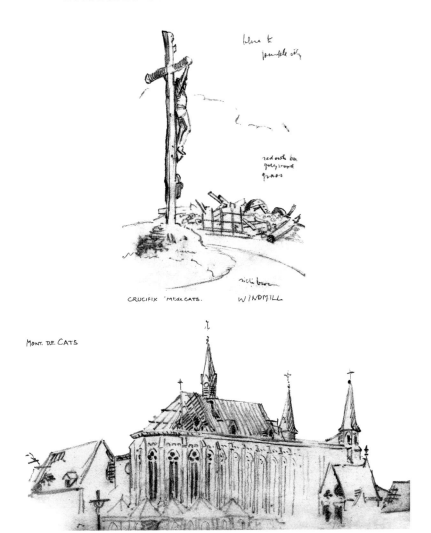

Flanders, July 1918, taken from Oakley's sketch book. (CR)

'This monastery on the hills between Belgium and France was a conspicuous landmark and it was not until 1918 that the Germans shelled it and the equally famous windmill.'

Lambert and Oakley joined the 32nd Division a few miles south-west of Ypres, not far from where they had been with the 23rd Division before it was sent to Italy. The tide of the German Spring Offensive had swept by but the area remained in British hands.

106

In March 1918 the Germans launched their Spring Offensive which was very successful at first, regaining in weeks all the ground which the British had taken two years to capture. But their supply lines and manpower resources were overstretched and troop morale was falling, partly because the Royal Navy's blockade of German ports made life at home very harsh for their families. The momentum slowed and the offensive was stopped by the end of July. In that month alone 250,000 American troops arrived in France and the build-up was accelerating. President Wilson had promised to raise 100 divisions – equivalent to about 2 million troops. (American divisions were much larger than British ones.) It was an irreversible turning point in the war and the Germans could only hope to keep fighting long enough to secure a negotiated ceasefire.

The Allies decided to attack on a broad front with massive concentrations of men and tanks, and to press forward relentlessly to allow the Germans no chance to regroup. It was the start of the Hundred Days Offensive which would end the war.

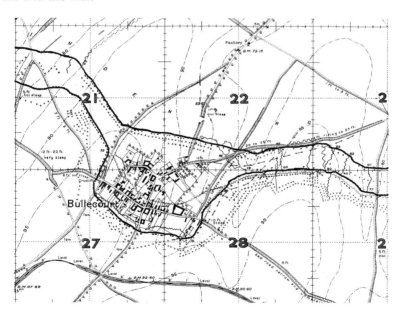

Map showing the position of the Hindenburg Line at Bullecourt. (JR/IWM)

Bullecourt was one of the villages on the old Somme battlefield which were re-fought over in the summer of 1918. The map shows how the Hindenburgh Line sometimes took in whole villages so that the buildings could be used for accommodation and storage.

The Hundred Days Offensive began with the Battle of Amiens on 8 August. On the British part of the front the spearhead troops were mainly provided by the Canadian and the Australian Corps. The 32nd Division was attached to the Canadian Corps for this battle and fought alongside the Canadian 1st, 2nd, 3rd and 4th Divisions. The battle was fought using tactics which the Australian General John Monash had used in capturing the village of Le Hamel: close co-ordination between infantry, tanks, artillery and aircraft, and no preliminary bombardment, to retain the element of surprise. The Canadian and the Australian Corps each gained about 6 miles, one of the greatest single-day advances of the war.

That defeat and the growing evidence in the field that German morale was collapsing led Ludendorff, the German commander, to call 8 August 'the black day of the German army'.

On 11 August Oakley wrote home to his mother:

> We have moved every day for the last 8 days sometimes twice a day, took part in the most successful show that the British Army has had. I have had all of the billeting and camp commandant's work to do as well as my own jobs. Very little sleep but am perfectly fit and life is full of interest. I am writing this in an old Bosche head quarters which he left in a hurry. The village is in ruins and I am lucky to have four walls and a ceiling about the only room in the village that isn't missing something. I cant tell you about the operations and the battle but you can read it in the papers.

Scenes from the Battle of Amiens, August 1918. (CR)

'Some silhouette impressions on the battlefield during the recent British advance'. (ILN/ME)

AMIENS-PERONNE ROAD

REMAINS OF LIHONS

SOMME

Left: 'This was a lookout but shelled when I was looking at it'.
Right: 'The Cathedral of Corbie-sur-Somme. The interior was gutted.' (CR)

With the Canadian Corps, early to mid–August 1918.

The Australian Corps had its headquarters in the village of Vraignes. (CR)

For the second battle at Albert the 32nd Division was attached to the Australian Corps. There were five Australian divisions – enough for a full-sized corps – but one was being rested and the 32nd fought with the other four Australian divisions. They again gained all their objectives. After the battle, Oakley wrote to his brother Richard and said that there were 4,000 'birds' in their POW cage and told this story:

> A group of nine Argyll & Sutherland Highlanders from the 32nd Division got lost when 'going over' and got mixed up with some Australian soldiers who directed them back to their own unit on a route through a wood. Six of the Argylls were 'outed' by a machine gun before they got to the wood but the other three made it and went on until they came across a group of about 50 German soldiers with one officer. The senior private decided that the best thing to do was to shoot the officer, which they did. The other Germans promptly surrendered. When they were brought back to the British lines and interrogated they said they thought they had been attacked by more than three Argylls.

It sounds like a soldier's story and may well be exaggerated but in essence it is consistent with other evidence of low German morale.

AUG 1918 Australian Squadron RFO
Here Von Richthofen was brought down

From Oakley's scrapbook, August 1918. (CR)

Sketches and photographs taken with the Australian Corps during the Battle of Albert. Manfred von Richthofen, the Red Baron, had been brought down a few miles south of Albert on 21 April, probably by groundfire from Australian troops then in the area.

Silhouettes cut from sketches taken during the Battle of Albert, August 1918. (ILN/ME)

Captured German gun at St Quentin Canal. (CR)

'British 6 inch guns at St. Quentin Canal.' (ILN/ME)

The next phase of the offensive was to retake the German fortifications along the Hindenburg Line. For the Battle of St Quentin Canal which started on 29 September and for the rest of the war, the 32nd Division fought in the British IX Corps. Fighting alongside the Australian Corps they broke through along a 10-mile front.

'I shared a hut with a Scots officer who played the pipes'. (CR)

Mule limbers taking ammunition. (CR)

The Hundred Days Offensive was a series of short but intense battles in between which the Allies and Americans advanced into territory as the Germans withdrew, often with little resistance. (America was not an ally, she was an 'associated power' because an alliance with Britain, France and Belgium – all great colonial powers – would not have been acceptable to public opinion there.) Having crossed the Hindenburg Line, the 32nd Division marched rapidly eastwards past the villages of Nauroy and Joncourt and on to the small town of Bohain.

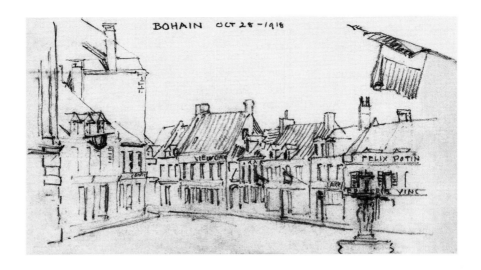

Pencil sketch of the centre of Bohain. (CR)

The small town of Bohain in Picardy was retaken on 18 October. There was then a pause in the advance for about three weeks while preparations were made for the last major battle of the war, the crossing of the River Sambre. On 27 October Oakley wrote to his mother about the reception they received in Bohain:

There were about 3,000 people left in the town when the Hun evacuated it. We were not the first troops in so I cant give you a description of their welcome but even when we moved up here everyone bowed and smiled and shook you by the hand. The British authorities are feeding the people and a queue forms up for hours in front of our HQ where the office is.

The first day an old lady came to our interpreter and asked whether the rations she had been given were really for a day or had she made a mistake and were they a week's rations she did not like to eat them in case they had to last for 7 days.

Each day we have the massed pipes – 40 pipes and 20 drums – in the village square at 4.30 pm and the streets are lined with civilians and soldiers. Today they had a special service in the parish church and the General and Staff and regimental officers and RC soldiers attended. The church was full and the service though in French and Latin was most impressive. 'Marseillaise' 'Ave Marie' 'Nat. Anthem' the sermon was very dramatic as much as I could understand.

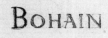 

BOHAIN   OCT· 1918

Le Général Commandant la 32ᵐᵉ Division Britannique a été profondément touché par le don si délicat de Madame Miau. Il lui en exprime ses remerciements personnels les plus vifs et les plus sincères. Il l'en remercie également au nom de la Nation et de l'Armée Britannique dont il est l'interprète autorisé. Il tient à lui dire qu'il conservera précieusement ce témoignage offert par une grande française comme le signe le plus émouvant et très expressif des sentiments de reconnaissance et de parfaite cordialité de la population française de Bohain à l'égard des troupes Britanniques.

29. 10. 1918.

Address of thanks for the friendship and hospitality received from the people of Bohain. (JR)

Afterwards you might have seen a French officer and the curé followed by the ADC with Monsieur le Marie in top hat and a tricolour round his middle and a lady like Mrs Hardcastle on either side of him going down the town. The Marie bowing and raising his hat to everyone and the ADC returning salutes from the soldiers. The lady meanwhile hugging a parcel to her breast.

Oakley's letter went on:

On arrival at our residence the port was passed around and the lady made a touching little speech and presented a piece of needlework to the General which she had worked on the quiet for 4 years and intended to give to the first General who should come to the town. She had altered the date 3 times but her faith was justified at last.

We returned the call at 6pm and found the Marie and 8 aldermen or councillors with the curé and Madame Miau seated round a table with champagne and cognac in clay besmirched bottles. After reading a lengthy peroration in French and presenting a bouquet with tricolour ribbon to the General he replied in his best French.

Tomorrow we are entertaining the Marie and curé to dinner.

Major A.H.S. Waters VC (left) and Lieutenant Colonel J.N. Marshall VC (right).
(HLOC/ME)

Before the Germans left the town they set fire to the Hotel de Ville and took all the farmers' livestock.

The Battle of Sambre began on 4 November, a week before the ceasefire. The key task was to force a crossing of the River Sambre and its continuation, the Sambre–Oise Canal.

The 32nd Division crossed at the Ors section of the canal. They won four VCs on the first day. The Division's Royal Engineers had to construct pontoons and repair bridges under heavy fire. Their commander Major A.H.S. Waters (left) and Sapper A. Archibald were awarded VCs and both survived. Second Lieutenant J. Kirk of the 2nd Manchesters and Lieutenant Colonel J.N. Marshall (right), the CO of the 16th Lancashire Fusiliers, were killed and awarded posthumous VCs. Marshall's gazetted rank when he died was Lieutenant but he had been promoted rapidly in the field and wounded ten times in previous engagements.

The poet Wilfred Owen, a Lieutenant serving in the 2nd Manchesters, was also killed on the canal on 4 November 1918. The Latin saying *Dulce et decorum est pro patria mori* (roughly: It is sweet and fitting to die for one's country) was widely used in Britain as a mark of respect for soldiers who had done just that. Owen used *Dulce et Decorum Est* as the title of one of his poems, but ended:

The old Lie; Dulce et Decorum est
Pro Patria Mori.

During the last phase of the war, the Germans concentrated their efforts on defending positions where machine guns could be used to best effect. The idea was to inflict maximum casualties on the attackers and give their infantry time to retreat to the next defensible position with the fewest possible casualties. It was a very effective tactic. Many more Allied soldiers were killed than German soldiers. When the defending machine-gunners had held off an attack for as long as possible, they surrendered. But that was not an option for attacking troops trying to cross a river or canal.

On Armistice Day, Oakley wrote to his brother Richard about the battle:

> Well we finished up with a great battle a few days ago, across the canal and I visited the place where they crossed the next day. Mannie's lot had a fairly easy time and got across with few casualties and captured about 100 machine gunners on the other bank, but the Lancashire Brigade were held up for a long time and a lot of casualties occurred near the foot bridges among the R.Es, Pioneers and Lancs Fusiliers.
>
> I saw 30 dead around one bridge, one poor fellow half way across. I regret to say Lt. Col Marshall MC with 10 wound stripes and 2 rows of decorations was killed crossing at the head of his Battn. I went to his funeral later.
>
> The bridges were made of floats and some foot bridges of the Boches were repaired.

The letter went on to explain that at the place where Mannie's lot – the Dorsets – crossed, the banks of the canal stood several feet above the surrounding ground and thus provided good cover for troops assembling to cross. In contrast, at the place where the Lancashires crossed the banks were much lower, leaving their troops more vulnerable to enemy machine-gun fire.

Richard had served in the Machine Gun Corps and would have understood perfectly.

Kirk, Marshall and Owen are buried in the Ors Communal Cemetery 3 miles south-west of Landrecies.

AVESNES
NOV 9·1918·

'Where we finished the war'.
Avesnes-sur-Helpe. (CR)

After crossing the Sambre–Oise Canal, the 32nd Division pushed on to the small town of Avesnes-sur-Helpe on 8 November. This is Oakley's account in a letter to his sister Margaret:

We are nearing the end now and today we made a triumphal entry into A —— surrounded by French kiddies with red white and blue flags and streamers, then came the General and me carrying three bouquets of flowers and a flag on my horse's head which unfortunately had a brass point which caught my nose as I bent to the acclamation of the populace and consequently my nose bled profusely during the ceremony.

We advanced to the Marie and were received on the steps by the Marie and Corporation, presented with a bouquet and went in to drink a glass of champagne.

An English lady was presented to the General and others shook hands and the *Marie* (Mayor) kissed him on both cheeks. I avoided kissing with the aid of the flowers and a bloody nose. We then marched through the chief streets the pipes playing 'Heilan Lassie' and so to the outskirts of the town. A regular Lord Mayor's procession Nov. 9th what? [A reference to Military Sunday in York.]

DIMANCHE 10 Novembre 1918 — SEIZIÈME ANNÉE — N° 2091

L'Avenir Libéral

Journal Indépendant de l'Arrondissement d'Avesnes

Rédaction et Administration   6   Avenue de la Gare   6   Avesnes-sur-Helpe

RÉCEPTION DE L'ÉTAT-MAJOR ANGLAIS.

AVIS A NOS LECTEURS

L'Avenir Libéral reparaît après le long silence que les douloureux événements de ces dernières années lui ont imposé.

Respectueux des lois et règlements qui régissent, en ce moment, la presse, nous bornerons provisoirement notre rôle à publier fidèlement les communiqués officiels et à renseigner nos lecteurs sur les faits locaux et régionaux, qui ne manqueront pas d'intérêt pour eux.

On ne s'attend naturellement pas de nous, en ce moment, des appréciations sur les événements présents ou passés. Notre rôle ne peut être celui là.

Par la suite, notre Conseil de Direction aura la charge de régler l'orientation à donner à notre propagande et de choisir ceux à qui il confiera la mission de la mener à bonne fin.

E. S-H.

OMNIBUS

C'est samedi ! Présent — Du papier, S. V. P. — D'ailleurs que vous dire, que vous ne le pensiez ? — L'égoïsme heureux — Fûtes-vous comme moi ? — Le bonheur des autres.

Sans un coup de téléphone, sans le moindre télégramme, ni la plus petite lettre d'avis, me voici à mon poste.

C'est samedi, le journal paraît, « ON » est là !

Mais je suis prévenu d'être très court et de vous dire pourquoi.

La raison est simple comme bonjour : notre fabricant de papier a complètement oublié ses marchés et il laisse notre magasin vide.

Nous sommes réduits, jusqu'à ce que cet honorable industriel vienne à récépiscence, à la portion congrue : nous sommes rationnés, quoi !

Chers lecteurs, contentez-vous donc pour aujourd'hui, d'un modeste in-quarto et attendez vous à la récidive pour quelques numéros encore.

D'ailleurs, que vous dirais-je ? Vous sent z tous ce que je pourrais écrire. Vous êtes tous très heureux, comme je le suis moi-même et vous chantez la délivrance. Ma voix fait chorus et ma plume également.

Mais, si vous le voulez bien, je vous suggérerai une pensée, une seule : Nous sommes tous enchantés et il y a vraiment de quoi, mais êtes-vous comme moi ?

J'ai été longtemps, une demi-heure, une heure, plus peut-être, à me dire, in petto, à songer à mes frères, parents amis et connaissances : quel bonheur ! quel bonheur d'être enfin délivrés ! oui, j'ai été longtemps, très également heureux, de penser que d'autres n'avaient pas la même chance que nous.

Je me repens sincèrement de ce mouvement involontaire et je m'en excuse envers tous ceux qui subissent encore l'occupation ennemie. Puissent-ils y bien vite de ce bienfait que nous apprécions tous ici : sentir leur poitrine soulagée du poids de la botte allemande.

Dites? Soyez sincères ! Vous avez pensé comme moi, mais, au plus vite, aussi, votre cœur est allé aux autres occupés.

Dieu veuille, n'est-ce pas, que nous nous réjouissions au plus tôt de leur bonheur, à eux aussi......

— Vous allez être trop long !

— Hélas ! Que de choses j'aurais pourtant encore à dire !

— Bah ! L'Avenir — sans jeu de mot — est là !
ON ?

Le 9 Octobre 1918.

L'Etat-Major Anglais à Avesnes

Après une nuit et une matinée angoissantes, nous voyions, vendredi à 1 heure, entrer en ville les premiers soldats anglais.

Ils étaient accueillis en libérateurs par la population.

Bien des larmes d'émotion coulèrent et de toutes les poitrines s'échappèrent des soupirs de satisfaction.

En un clin d'œil, les rues étaient pavoisées. Nos trois couleurs soulignaient de leur éclat, les traces de dévastation, causées par les explosions et les obus.

Dès vendredi soir, M. le général de brigade Armytage qu'avait précédé l'interprète Ludovic de Bray, attaché à sa brigade, visitait M. Moity, Maire et recevait de lui, avec satisfaction, l'assurance que tous les services municipaux étaient restés parfaitement organisés et que la ville était apte à recevoir l'état-major du général Lambert.

Samedi à midi, cet état-major nous arrivait et une réception charmante lui était faite par la municipalité.

Les fleurs étaient de la partie et la coupe traditionnelle de

The local newssheet reporting on the liberation of Avesnes. (JR)

In April 1919 the Mayor led a deputation to visit the 32nd Division which was then based in Bonn, to thank them again for their part in the liberation of the town (page 147).

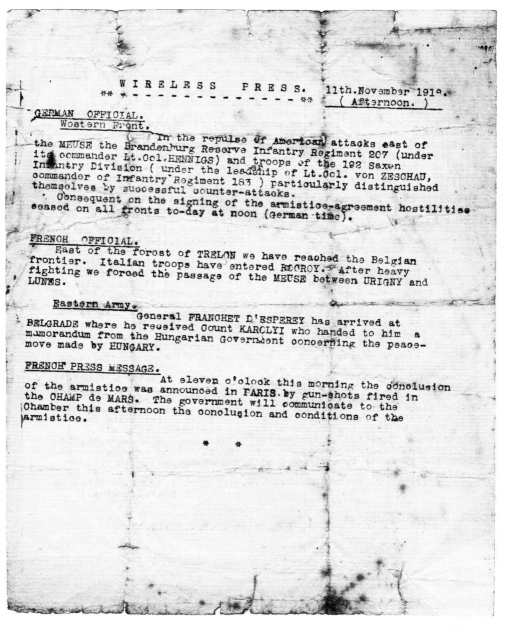

WIRELESS PRESS. 11th.November 1918.
** ------------------ ** (Afternoon.)

GERMAN OFFICIAL.
  Western Front.
          In the repulse of American attacks east of
the MEUSE the Brandenburg Reserve Infantry Regiment 207 (under
its commander Lt.Col.HENNIGS) and troops of the 192 Saxon
Infantry Division (under the leadship of Lt.Col. von ZESCHAU,
commander of Infantry Regiment 183) particularly distinguished
themselves by successful counter-attacks.
    Consequent on the signing of the armistice-agreement hostilities
ceased on all fronts to-day at noon (German time).

FRENCH OFFICIAL.
    East of the forest of TRELON we have reached the Belgian
frontier. Italian troops have entered ROCROY. After heavy
fighting we forced the passage of the MEUSE between URIGNY and
LUNES.

    Eastern Army.
          General FRANCHET D'ESPEREY has arrived at
BELGRADE where he received Count KAROLYI who handed to him a
memorandum from the Hungarian Government concerning the peace-
move made by HUNGARY.

FRENCH PRESS MESSAGE.
          At eleven o'clock this morning the conclusion
of the armistice was announced in PARIS by gun-shots fired in
the CHAMP de MARS. The government will communicate to the
Chamber this afternoon the conclusion and conditions of the
armistice.

              *   *

(JR)

This page and the one opposite are both sides of the 32nd Division's daily newssheet for 12 November 1918, with details of the Armistice.

```
        W I R E L E S S   P R E S S.        12th November 1918.
        * * - - - - - - - - - - - * *         ( Morning. )

FRENCH OFFICIAL.
     In the 52nd. month of a war unprecedented in history the
French Army, with the aid of her Allies, has consummated the defeat
of the enemy.   Our troops, animated by the purest spirit of sacri-
fice and, during four years of unbroken fighting, giving an example
of sublime endurance and daily heroism, have fulfilled the task
confided to them by the fatherland.  Now, sustaining with unyield-
ing energy the enemy attacks, and now, attacking themselves and
forcing victory, they have after four months' decisive offensive
hustled, defeated and thrown out of France the mighty German Army,
and compelled it to ask for peace.  All the conditions required for
the suspension of hostilities having been accepted by the enemy
the armistice came into operation to-day at eleven o'clock.
ITALIAN  OFFICIAL.    Our troops have reached the BRENNER.
In the operations extending from Oct.24 to 3 p.m., Nov.4 our captures
now ascertained amounted to 10,658 officers, 416,116 other ranks,
6818 guns.        Consequent on the conclusion of the armistice with
Germany operations were suspended on all fronts at 11a.m. Nov.11th.
BRITISH PRESS MESSAGE.   The news of the signing of the armistice
was made known to the general public in LONDON at 11 o'clock by
the firing of the maroons used in air-raid warnings. The Prime
Minister addressing the crowd in Downing St., said, "The people of
this Empire with their allies have won a great victory.  It is the
sons and daughters of the Empire who have done it.  It is a victory
greater than has ever been known in history.  Let us thank God!"
The Prime Minister in the House of Commons read the terms of the
armistice. They include:-The immediate evacuation of BELGIUM, ALSACE
LORRAINE, and LUXEMBURG. The evacuation by the enemy of the Rhine
lands, to be completed within 30 days. Railways of ALSACE-LORRAINE
to be handed over.  All German troops in RUSSIA, RUMANIA and else-
where to be withdrawn.  Immediate repatriation of allied and
United States prisoners without reciprocity.  Complete abandonment
of the Treaties of BUCHAREST and BREST-LITOWSK.  Immediate cessat-
ion of all hostilities on the sea.  The handing over of all
submarines.  Duration of the armistice 36 days.  5000 guns, 30,000
machineguns, 3000 trench-mortars, 2000 aeroplanes to be surrendered.
Black Sea ports to be evacuated by the Germans.  All material
seized by Germany to be abandoned and all allied ships seized by
Germany are to be returned............(Report incomplete owing to
                                             heavy jamming.)


LATE GERMAN OFFICIAL.
     "Omitted".(Announced by BERLIN at 19.30., 11/11/18.)

                    *  *  *
```

(JR)

The wear on Oakley's copy suggests that it may have passed through many hands. Having the news in print was tangible evidence that the war really was over.

```
■ DIVISIONAL HEADQUARTERS.
    G.O.C.                    Maj.-Gen. T.S.Lambert, C.B.,C.M.G.
    A.D.C.                    Lieut. H.L.Oakley.
    A.D.C.& Camp Com.         Major H.C.Meredith.
    G.S.O. I.                 Lt.-Col. E.FitzG.Dillon, D.S.O.
    G.S.O. II.                Major J.Y.C.Eyld, D.S.O., M.C.
    G.S.O. III.               Captain E.B.P.Speed, M.C.
    A.A. & Q.M.G.             Lt.-Col. J.F.E.Robinson, D.S.O.
    D.A.A.G.                  Major G.H.Teall, D.S.O.
    D.A.Q.M.G.                Major G.J.Aris, D.S.O.
    D.A.D.V.S.                Major G.B.C.Rees-Mogg.
    D.A.D.O.S.                Major L.E.Purchas.
    D.A.P.M.                  Captain G.E.Corrall.

■ 32ND DIVISIONAL ARTILLERY.
    C.R.A.                    Brig.-Gen. J.A.Tyler, C.M.G.
    Brigade-Major.            Major A.H.Burne, D.S.O.
    Staff Captain.            Lieut. A.G.Eaddy.
    161 Bde., R.F.A.          Lt.-Col. H.H.Hulton, D.S.O.
    168 Bde., R.F.A.          Lt.-Col. G.N.B.Carrington, D.S.O.
    D.A.C.                    Lt.-Col. J.Walker, D.S.O.

■ 32ND DIVISIONAL ENGINEERS.
    C.R.E.                    Lt.-Col. O.C.Pollard, C.M.G.,D.S.O.
    Adjutant.                 Captain P.B.Coulthurst.
    206 Field Coy.            Major J.M.MacIver.
    218 Field Coy.            Major A.H.S.Waters, D.S.O., M.C.
    219 Field Coy.            Major E.D.Moore.

■ MEDICAL SERVICES.
    A.D.M.S.                  Colonel E.Bennett, D.S.O.
    D.A.D.M.S.                Major L.Anderson, D.S.O.


◆ 14TH INFANTRY BRIGADE.
    G.O.C.                    Brig.-Gen. L.P.Evans, V.C., D.S.O.
    Brigade-Major.            Major R.F.H.Massey-Westropp.
    Staff Captain.            Captain E.C.Nicholson, M.C.

◆ 5/6th Royal Scots.
    O.C.                      Lt.-Col. J.A.Fraser, D.S.O.,D.C.M.
    a/2nd-in-Com.             A/Major J.Muir, D.S.O.
    Adjutant.                 Lieut. A.N.MacDonald, M.C.

◆ 1st Dorset Regt.
    O.C.                      Lt.-Col. H.D.Thwaytes, D.S.O.
    2nd-in-Comd.              Major C.H.Morris, M.C.
    A/Adjt.                   Captain E.L.Stephenson, M.C.

◆ 15th High.L.Infy.
    O.C.                      Lt.-Col. V.D.Ramsden, D.S.O., M.C.
    2nd-in-Comd.              A/Major J.F.Muir, M.C.
    A/Adjt.                   Captain J.E.Stephens, M.C.

◆ 14th T.M. Battery.
    O.C.                      Lieut. A.E.Classey.

        ■ 32nd Bn., M.G. Corps.
            O.C.              Lt.-Col. E.G.Aldous.
            a/2nd-in-Com.     Major W.Harrison, M.C.
            Adjutant.         Capt. A.J.C.Freshwater.

■ 90th Field Ambulance.
    O.C.                      Lt.-Col. G.M.Page.
```

Headquarters staff and senior officers of the 32nd Division. (JR)

▲ 96TH INFANTRY BRIGADE.
G.O.C.   Brig.-Gen. A.C.Girdwood, D.S.O.
Brigade-Major.   Captain I.H.Wake, M.C.
Staff Captain.   Captain A.C.Smith, M.C.

▲ 15th Lancs.Fusrs.
O.C.   Lt.-Col. C.E.R.C.Alban, D.S.O.
2nd-in-Comd.   Major L.C.Mandleberg, M.C.
A/Adjt.   Captain A.Healing, M.C.

▲ 16th Lancs.Fusrs.
O.C.   Lt.-Col. J.M.Marshall, M.C. *Compton Smith*
2nd-in-Comd.   Major F.E.Robathan.
A/Adjt.   Captain F.H.Watts.

▲ 2nd Manchester Regt.
O.C.   Lt.-Col. G.McM.Robertson, D.S.O.
2nd-in-Comd.   Major R.C.Wynter, M.C.
Adjutant.   Captain W.Kay, M.C.

▲ 96th T.M. Battery.
O.C.   Captain W.O.Smart.

■ 16th High.L.I.(Pioneers)
O.C.   Lt.-Col. F.Kyle, D.S.O.
2nd-in-Com.   Maj. W.D.Scott, DSO.,MC.
Adjutant.   Captain A.Macfarlane, M.C.

■ 91st Field Ambulance.
O.C.   Lt.-Col. F.G.Sampson, D.S.O.

● 97TH INFANTRY BRIGADE.
G.O.C.   Brig.-Gen. G.A.Armytage, C.M.G.,D.S.O.   *Book*
Brigade-Major.   Captain G.B.Groom, M.C.   *97*
Staff Captain.   Captain C.E.Framingham, M.C.   *Brux*

● 1/5th Border Regt.
O.C.   Lt.-Col. H.N.Vinen.
2nd-in-Comd.   A/Maj. J.Hassell, D.S.O., M.C.
A/Adjt.   Lieut. A.E.Knight.

● 2nd K.O.Y.L.I.
O.C.   Lt.-Col. L.Limmetts.   BROOKS
2nd-in-Comd.   Major A.W.Robinson.
A/Adjt.   Lieut. A.Pontefract.

● 10th A. & S. Highrs.
O.C.   Lt.-Col. H.G.Sotheby, D.S.O., M.V.O.
2nd-in-Comd.   Major N.McQueen, D.S.O.
A/Adjt.   Captain T.N.P.Eourston, M.C.

▲ 97th T.M. Battery.
O.C.   Captain M.W.Richmond, M.C.

■ 92nd Field Ambulance.
O.C.   Lt.-Col. W.L.Bradish, D.S.O.

The list has been corrected to late 1918. Lt-Col Marshall was killed
on 4 November 1918. (JR)

Chapter 7

Amusement by the Meuse

Oakley's Christmas card for the 32nd Division. (JR)

THE OCCUPATION OF BELGIUM

(JR)

After the Armistice the 32nd Division moved into Belgium with its headquarters in the Château de Bioul near the town of Annevoire on the Meuse. It was not yet certain that the ceasefire would hold so units had to maintain a degree of readiness. But there was time to relax and enjoy the hospitality of the Belgian people.

Oakley started to keep a photograph album recording scenes in and around the headquarters. They show a wide range of leisure activities and it is clear too that the officers had plenty of female company. General Lambert is sometimes shown with two escorts, as Oakley has caricatured him in this pen and wash cartoon.

Charades.
Oakley is
knitting. (JR)

Tobogganing. (JR)

127

Nanette GOC and
Hélène ADC. (JR)

The meet of the Annevoir Hunt. (JR)

Hélène. (JR)

Jimmy and the mascot of the
Royal Scots. (JR)

The two ladies Oakley has shown with Gen. Lambert in 'The Occupation of Belgium' cartoon on page 127 appear to be based on Nanette and Hélène.

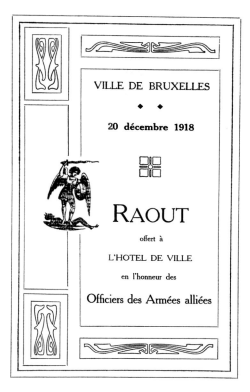

A celebratory concert in Brussels for Allied army officers. (JR)

CONCERT

donné dans la Salle du Conseil communal

par le corps de musique du

Ier RÉGIMENT DE GRENADIERS

Directeur : M. C. LECAIL, Inspecteur des Musiques de l'Armée

◎   ◎

PROGRAMME

PREMIÈRE PARTIE

1. **Marche et Chœur** extraits de la
   " Rubens-Cantate " . . . . . Peter Benoit.
   (Les cinq parties du monde.)

2. **Le dernier jour de la Terreur**. H. Litolff.
   (Drame symphonique.)

3. **Chu Chin Chow**, fragments du
   ballet-pantomime . . . . . . Fr. Norton.

4. **La Bohème**, transcription . . . G. Puccini.

5. **Chant Hindou** (Désespérance) . H. Bemberg.
   (Chanté par M. Floris Van Vracem.)

6. **Rhapsodie Congolaise** . . . . C. Lecail.

DEUXIÈME PARTIE

7. **Les Deux Pigeons**, ballet . . . A. Messager.
   1) Entrée des Tziganes; 2) Scène et Pas
   des Deux Pigeons; 3) Danse Slave;
   4) Finale.

8. **Historiette**. . . . . P. Lagasse.

9. *a)* **Love's Garden of Roses** . H. Wood.
   (Mélodie.)

   b) **O Flower divine** . . . . H. Wood.
   (Mélodie.)

10. Fantaisie sur l'opéra **Lakmé** . . Léo Delibes.

11. **Babil d'Oiseaux** . . . . . C. Lecail.
    (Bluette pour trois flûtes.)

12. **Stars and Stripes for ever**. J.-Ph. Sousa.
    (March).

LA BRABANÇONNE

N. B. Les hymnes nationaux des pays alliés seront exécutés à la fin de la première partie du concert (à 10 heures).

The Dump, Christmas 1918. (JR)

John Hassall's cover shows Hindenburg surrendering, but there is no triumphalism in victory.

THINGS I HAVE NEVER SEEN AT THE FRONT.

A Kirchener Girl tripping through Ypres.

A Transport Officer and a Quartermaster taking unnecessary exercise before breakfast.

An Army Commander lunching off bully beef and biscuits.

An Officer of G.H.Q. choosing and matching ribands.

Volunteers for a working party.

Specially drawn for THE DUMP *by H. L. Oakley.*

'Things I Have Never Seen at the Front', *The Dump*, Christmas 1918. (ILN/ME)

Oakley's contribution to the final edition of *The Dump*.

OUR GENERALS

From top left to bottom right: Brig.-Gen. J.A.Tyler, Royal Artillery; Brig.-Gen. L. Evans VC, 14th Infantry Brigade; Maj.-Gen. T.S. Lambert, 32nd Division; Brig.-Gen. A.C. Girdwood, 96th Infantry Brigade; and Brig.-Gen. Sir G. Armitage, Infantry Brigade. (JR)

The 'Our Generals' piece above and 'Some of our Lads' opposite were included in the souvenir programme of the 32nd Division's annual Christmas review. The portraits of the Generals are arranged in the shape of the emblem of the Division. In the programme itself the names of the Generals and the units were not given, perhaps because the information was still classified.

SOME OF OUR LADS

Composition of the 32nd Division during the final advance from Amiens to Avesnes. (JR)

14th Infantry Brigade: 5/6 Royal Scots, 1st Dorsets, 15th Highland
Light Infantry.
96th Infantry Brigade: 15th and 16th Lancashire Fusiliers, 2nd
Manchester Regiment.
97th Infantry Brigade: 1st King's Own Yorkshire Light Infantry,
11th Border Regiment, 10th Argyll and Sutherland Highlanders.
Each Brigade also had its own Trench Mortar Battery.

Services under Divisional control: Pioneers (16th Highland Light Infantry),
Royal Artillery, Royal Engineers, Machine Gun Corps, Medical and
Ambulance Services, and HQ staff.

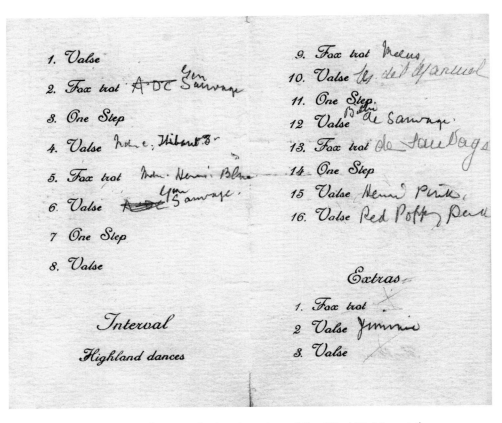

1. Valse
2. Fox trot A DC Sauvage
3. One Step
4. Valse how c. Hilbert B.
5. Fox trot Mon. Henri Bln
6. Valse Sauvage.
7 One Step
8. Valse

9. Fox trot Meeus
10. Valse de d'Arnual
11. One Step.
12 Valse de Sauvage.
13. Fox trot de Saulbags
14. One Step
15 Valse Henri Pink.
16. Valse Red Poff Parl

Interval

Highland dances

Extras

1. Fox trot
2 Valse Jimmie
3. Valse

A New Year's dance at the headquarters of the 32nd Division at the Château de Bioul. (JR)

It looks from the dance card as if Oakley had booked the second and sixth dances but then had been outflanked by a General. There was no General Sauvage in the British Army but he might have been French or Belgian. Another possibility is that the card belonged to General Lambert's escort and she was using a pet name for him.

The last panel of *The Bystander* piece opposite shows the Highland dances in the interval.

'Amusement by the Meuse' in *The Bystander*, 1918. (ILN/ME)

Scenes around the headquarters of the 32nd Division at Bioul in the Meuse valley.

The Prince of Wales (later King Edward VIII) visited the headquarters of the 32nd Division at Bioul in January 1919. Oakley took two portraits. The Prince signed and dated one copy of the full-length portrait and presented it to Gen. Lambert, who later gave it to Oakley. He sent the other copy home to his mother, Queen Mary.

The Prince of Wales (with cushion) talking to Gen. Lambert (sitting left). (JR)

In a letter to his mother after the visit, Oakley said:

The first afternoon we took him down to the chateau and had tea with the Countess de Meuse and her daughters and the three girls from Brussels staying with them. After tea we sang a bit and played animal grab and took a flashlight photo sitting on the hearth rug. I accompanied the Prince when he sang Polly wolly doodle.

The Prince of Wales at Château de Bioul, Belgium, 24 January 1919. (National Portrait Gallery, London (NPG))

This portrait was widely reproduced and became Oakley's best-known work. It is now in the National Portrait Gallery collection.

(1) A Patrol—CENSOR'S OPINION: "The men don't seem to be enjoying it enough"

(2) At G.H.Q.—CENSOR'S OPINION: "The Staff should never rest"

(3) An Issue of Rum—CENSOR'S OPINION: "Rum? Never!"

'As the Artist Might Have Drawn It', *The Bystander*, 29 January 1919. (ILN/ME)

Oakley kept only one example of work which the censor had disallowed, apart from a few blackings out of place names, so he was not much troubled by him.

'As the Censor Would Certainly Prefer It', *The Bystander*, 29 January 1919. (ILN/ME)

But the pervasive effect was always there and would have influenced how he portrayed things. And the censor was too good a target to miss for a bit of fun.

(MR)

(ILN/ME)

The top piece on this page was to have been the top section of the 'Proverbs for the Pushful' piece on page 66. But the censor crossed it out at proof stage so the page had to be pulled. Oakley then made the lower piece above to replace it and the page was published later.

Most of Oakley's work for *The Bystander* was done in naturalistic style, albeit often with an element of caricature, but some of it, including the Proverbs pieces, was done as cartoons. In that vein the deed of bashing the Germans – as Oakley depicts in the censored panel – might be said to be harmless. But the censor took it literally and struck it out because it was not acceptable to show British soldiers threatening German prisoners. So, in the new version Oakley showed them being kind instead.

Chapter 8

The Occupation of the Rhineland

32nd Division headquarters, Popplesdorfer Allee, Bonn. (JR)

Under the terms of the Armistice, the Rhineland was to be demilitarised and administered by the Allies. The 32nd Division was sent to Bonn in February 1919 as part of the British Army of Occupation. There had been no fighting on German soil during the war; and after fighting in France, Belgium and Italy, Oakley was pleased to be in Germany. He gave his first impressions in a letter to his mother dated 3 February:

> Just a line to say we are in Germany at last. We arrived yesterday after a two-day motor run and are installed at Bonn on the Rhine.
>
> We are in most sumptuous billets. The General and I and the Mess live with a Doctor. We have a marble stepped bathroom and hot water laid on in our rooms. Everything is very modern, hot water pipes, electric lights near my bed and on this table. Thickly carpeted floor and pillows of needlework etc. We are in Popplesdorfer Alee a large Boulevarde in the most swagger part of town. It is freezing hard outside.
>
> The Boche is fairly obsequious and wishes to do us well but one can't trust their ugly faces and square heads. The ladies I think would like to fraternise but we are not allowed to speak to them in public though in one's billet one can be polite.
>
> I think we shall be very happy then.

'My bedroom in Popplesdorfer Alee. The Prince of Wales is on the wall'. (JR)

'Poppleton of Popplesdorf. A play on Oakley's home village near York and the HQ address on Popplesdorfer Alee'. (JR)

'Caught in the Act … Fraternisation *Verboten*'. (JR)

'Fraulines in Bonn: Kathe (left) and Erna (right).'. (JR)

'An ADC is not always necessary'. (JR)

'Nobody's Children in Neutral Zone'. (JR)

'My Mess Coporal and servant, Clarence Brown'. (JR)

'Headquarters staff of the 32nd Division, Bonn, March 1919'. Front row: Col Harrison; Brig.-Gen. Tyler; Maj.-Gen. Lambert; Lt-Col J.F. Robinson; Maj. G.H. Teall. Oakley is standing in the back row, first left. (CR)

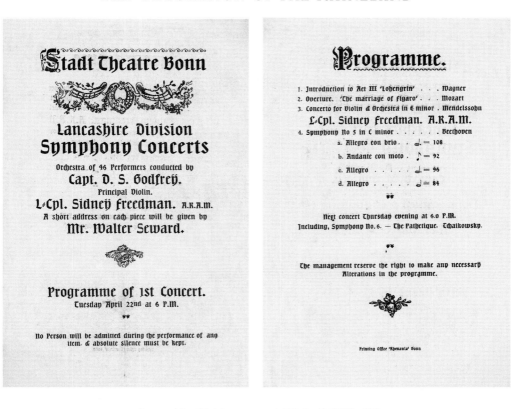

Lancashire Division concert, 22 April 1919. (JR)

The 32nd Division was sometimes known informally as the Lancashire Division even though not all of its units came from there. The use of the name for this concert may also have been a tribute to the 2nd Manchesters and the 16th Lancashire Fusiliers, who had distinguished themselves at the Battle of Sambre.

Captain D.S. Godfrey was the son of Dan Godfrey, the conductor of the Bournemouth Symphony Orchestra who established its reputation among the leading British orchestras. In the staff portrait opposite, Godfrey is standing in the back row, third from the left.

Two days later there was a second concert featuring Carl Schaefer playing cello variations, and there was a third concert on 29 April. The value of these concerts would have been partly as entertainment for the occupying army but also as bridge building towards peace. All of the music at this concert was by German composers.

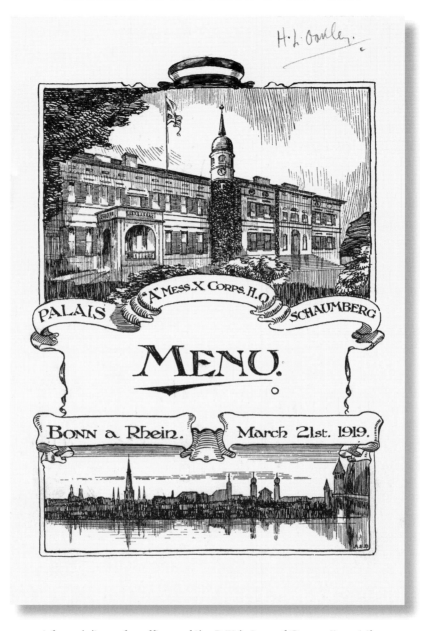

A formal dinner for officers of the British Amy of Occupation at the
Schaumberg Palace. (JR)

This menu card (not by Oakley) was not intended for propaganda
purposes, but the symbolism is clear enough.

Oakley's sketch of the lady from the image below, sitting second from right. (CR)

(CR)

In April 1919, the Mayor and senior citizens of Avesnes in France came to Bonn to express their friendship and gratitude towards the 32nd Division for their part in the liberation of the town the previous November. There was a parade, an exchange of banners (Oakley is holding one on the left) and a dinner.

147

Boulogne ... (JR)

Blighty ... (JR)

... and then
Demobbed.

Capt. H.L. Oakley, May 1919. (JR)

Oakley was appointed MBE (Military Division) for his work as ADC to
Gen. Lambert.

Chapter 9

From War to Peace

" Christmas in Rhineland "

SILHOUETTES BY H. L. OAKLEY

Oakley was home but the British Army stayed in the Rhineland. (ILN/ME)

Oakley had a lucky war, not only surviving without injury but also being able to carry on with his silhouette work. With the two recruiting posters, *The Bystander* column and the portrait of the Prince of Wales, his career as an artist had developed faster than it might have done without the war. So he had no hesitation about what to do when he got home. He went straight back to his pre-war routine of spending the summer in Harrogate and Scarborough and then going to London for the winter.

But he had not finished with the war yet. The British Army remained in the Rhineland for several years and *The Bystander* continued to cover events there with a regular column 'The Bystander in Occupation', written by Eric Gordon and illustrated by Oakley. Gordon was based in Cologne but Oakley did the illustrations in England, sometimes with the aid of photographs sent by Gordon. He knew the Rhineland from his own time there and he could 'do' the German character.

The column generally took a humorous or tongue-in-cheek look at the interactions between the Army and the local population. But it sometimes dealt with more serious topics.

Allowances of food are almost at starvation levels. (ILN/ME)

The first priority was to restore adequate food supplies. In the last months of the war, German soldiers had been on short rations but their families at home were much worse off. The blockade of German ports by the Royal Navy had been lifted but it took several months to restore supplies. Many British units made a direct contribution by giving up part of their own rations for the local population.

The 'Bystander in Occupation' column opposite celebrates the signing of the Treaty of Versailles and the lifting of the ban on fraternising with the enemy.

378   The Bystander, August 6, 1919

PEACE brings her penalties, no less disliked than War's. The actual signature of the Treaty was suitably celebrated in Cologne, officially by the firing of a hundred and one guns across the Rhine—the first, and the last, British guns to fire on German soil —and, unofficially, by slight additions to the performances in several cabarets—additions not always arranged by the German management, but received with equanimity

In COLOGNE

BY THE BYSTANDER IN OCCUPATION

official ban on "fraternising in public with the enemy." This was inevitable, not only because " the enemy " had officially ceased to exist, but, because the influx of Allied civilians of both sexes into Cologne, the only reason for whose advent was to enter into more or less friendly

" Performances in several cabarets "

by the mixed audience. Naturally, the Hun was not very exuberant. A few individuals, of the type which finds an excuse for drowning its sorrows as welcome as one for celebrating its successes, were, of course, in evidence, but on the whole, the note struck was one of hopeless resignation, tempered with relief that active operations were not to be resumed. The Boche had realised for several days that it was to be Peace—of our own, undiluted, original brand —or more War.

THE menacing procession of tanks which parked for a while before the Dom, *en route* for the bridgehead area, gave a chill of realism to those hotheads who had been in favour of throwing down the cards and refusing to play, in the hope of involving the Allies in a glorious mess.

THE realisation of the penalties of Peace is not confined to the Hun, however. First and foremost, in its consequences, was the removal of the

relations with the Rhinelander was beginning to make the order difficult to enforce, distinctly unpopular with the soldier, who was penalised by his khaki coat, and rather ridiculous.

BUT no more bitter blow could have been dealt to a possible Anglo-German *rapprochement* than the rescinding of this order. The salt has gone out of the fraterniser's life. No more does he thrill at whispering to his comrades in crime the addresses of cafés believed to be unknown to the A.P.M.; no more does the gay subaltern follow, with ostentatious nonchalance, fifty yards behind a Cologne damsel ; no more does the gilded staff unaccountably forsake the

Rolls-Royce for a seat in a crowded civilian train, bound for a quiet country village where the P.M. ceased from troubling and the " fratter " was at rest. The Rhine-madel, from being a delicious, forbidden, secret thing, at whom to wink was peril, and to smile to court disaster, has become merely a girl who probably cannot speak a word of your language, and whose attractions have to stand comparison with those of the numerous British girls now thronging Cologne.

NO one suffers more from the legalising of " fratting " than the Bystander in Occupation. Not that he ever indulged in the pastime. Even had he not been inspired by the proper national spirit of undying hatred of every individual, man, woman, or child born even twenty yards this side of the French and Belgian frontiers, his arduous labours on your behalf left him no time for such frivolity. No—his trouble is deeper seated—it threatens his very existence. Where can he find cheap humour in life on the Rhine, now that he will hear no more stories of how the A.P.M. has been dumbfounded by cunning " fratters," or the latter brought to book by the former and his gallant sleuths ? His heart is heavy over the prospective lack of copy, and it only requires a G.R.O. forbidding any reference to the " Boche " or the " Hun," and ordering this person to be in future referred to as " our late enemy," to lead him to select the highest of the local bridges and end a hopeless existence in the rushing waters of the Rhine.

ERIC GORDON

" The numerous British girls now thronging Cologne "

The Bystander in Occupation, *6 August 1919.* (ILN/ME)

The ban on fraternisation is lifted and spoils the fun for some.

Studio advertisement for Harrogate, 1919. (HLOC/ME)

Interior of Oakley's studio, 1919. (JR)

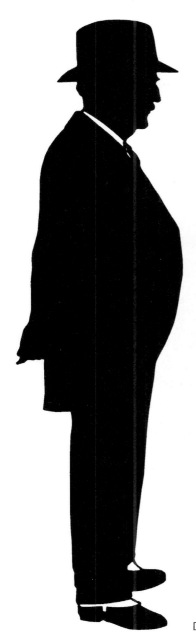

Dr Henry Hind of Harrogate. (HLOC/ME)

Dr Hind's portrait is on the left of the mantleshelf. The picture on the right, of a barmaid serving a customer, is the last scene on page 155, without the dog. The shield of the German imperial eagle is a trophy from Bonn.

'The Season in Harrogate in Silhouette', *The Bystander*, 10 September 1919. (ILN/ME)

'The Season in Harrogate in Silhouette', *The Bystander*, 10 September 1919. (ILN/ME)

Kaiser Wilhelm II was forced to abdicate just before the end of the war and went to live in Holland, first in Amerongen and then in Doorn, where he died in 1941.

When Oakley had shut his studio in Scarborough in 1914 he left a note on his studio door, saying, 'Off to silhouette the Kaiser'. It was only mock bravado of course but he did receive a letter from the ex-Kaiser after the war. It is not known whether the letter survives but Oakley had a list of unsolicited testimonials, which he pinned up in his studios. One entry reads:

The ex-Kaiser writing from Amarongen states: 'If I had made as good use of Scraps of Paper as you do, there would have been no war.'

The letter must have been written before Wilhelm moved from Amerongen in June 1919. He would have had access to English magazines in his exile and possibly even during the war. Oakley's work showed no bitterness towards the Germans and he was especially skillful in portraying horses, which may have appealed to the ex-Kaiser. He now had plenty of time on his hands and it is not too surprising that he wrote to Oakley. But what did he mean by making as good use of scraps of paper as Oakley did?

Some historians regard the numerous treaties and agreements between European countries to come to each others aid if they were attacked as an important factor in the escalation of the war. The assassination of Archduke Ferdinand set off a chain reaction. As more countries became involved, they triggered further interventions. Perhaps Wilhelm was alluding to those treaties as scraps of paper and implicitly acknowledging that there was a better way for Germany to have dealt with the situation.

But whatever he meant, any feelings of regret or remorse he may have had did not last. In 1940, when the German Army entered Paris, he sent a telegram of congratulations to Hitler.

When Oakley returned to Scarborough in the summer of 1919 he professed to be disappointed to find that his note was no longer on the door of his studio.

" Our Late Enemy "

' The Glances of the English Girls"

" Our former good friend, the Field Cashier '

Selection of Oakley's illustrations for 'The Bystander in Occupation'. (ILN/ME)

'Christmas Dances in Silhouette', *The Bystander Annual*, 1919. (ILN/ME)

'Woman's advance in the course of the last two hundred years to a recognised "equality", socially and politically, with man is manifest even in so superficial thing as the dance, and the exaggerated "courtliness" in the manners of the Eighteenth century has been superseded by an infinitely healthier comradeship.'

Gentlemen in formal dress. (HLOC/ME)

The Charm of the Silhouette

H. L. OAKLEY,
M.B.E., A.R.C.A.,

the famous Silhouette Artist, is in attendance daily, 10 a.m. to 6 p.m., in the Art Salon, 2nd Floor.

Silhouette Portraits make charming Christmas Cards, or can be mounted to form a Calendar.

BRAINS

SCISSORS

SKILL

FEES as follows:

2/6 for 2 Copies		Head and Shoulders.
5/- „ 2	„	Children's full length.
5/- „ 2	„	Adult's full Length.
7/6 „ 2	„	Dog's Portraits.

ART
SALON
Phone ONE Bournemouth.

In the summer of 1920, Oakley worked for the first time in Bournemouth.
(HLOC/ME)

Edward German, Edward Elgar, Alexander MacKenzie, Henry Wood and Dan Godfrey. (ILN/ME)

Taking the portrait of a child at a bazaar in Bournemouth, 1920. (JR)

At a one-day charity event like this Oakley reckoned on taking fifty to sixty portraits.

(CR)

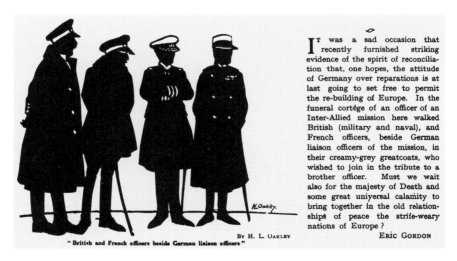

IT was a sad occasion that recently furnished striking evidence of the spirit of reconciliation that, one hopes, the attitude of Germany over reparations is at last going to set free to permit the re-building of Europe. In the funeral cortége of an officer of an Inter-Allied mission here walked British (military and naval), and French officers, beside German liaison officers of the mission, in their creamy-grey greatcoats, who wished to join in the tribute to a brother officer. Must we wait also for the majesty of Death and some great universal calamity to bring together in the old relationships of peace the strife-weary nations of Europe ?

ERIC GORDON

BY H. L. OAKLEY

"British and French officers beside German liaison officers"

The Bystander in Occupation, 13 March 1921. (ILN/ME)

The burial of a British officer in Cologne military cemetery became an act of reconciliation between Allied and German officers. The officer with an X on his greatcoat is the Kommandant of the Cologne garrison. The *Picklehaube* helmet had been replaced by the *Stahlhelm* for battlefield use, but senior officers still wore them on ceremonial occasions.

162

LEAGUES OF NATIONS

BY THE BYSTANDER IN OCCUPATION

"The O.C. Marriage"

THERE is said to be hidden in the deepest recesses of the Excelsior Hotel a mysterious person whose word is law to every registrar in Cologne, and who is known to them as the "Englischer Heirats Offizier"—the O.C. Marriages. They have never seen him, this Cupid Militant, but picture him to themselves as of mild disposition, since it is before him that soldiers about to commit matrimony with the late enemy come and swear oaths.

IT was not at this bureau of Love, G.H.Q., that the Bystander in Occupation learnt some details concerning the formation of local Leagues of Nations, but from a regimental officer who had been detailed to see the knot safely tied for one of his own men.

"ARMED," he said, "with the swear-paper, with permissions and declarations galore, including certificates that Blenkins' matrimonial past had either never existed or that he had got a proper discharge from it, I paraded and inspected him before he faced the Hun for the last time.

" 'A small S.D.R. ration 'ud come in 'andy, sir,' he murmured. 'I 'ad more 'eart in me at Mametz Wood than I 'ave for this raid.'

"WHEN I saw him next at the register office the old fighting spirit seemed to have come back. He kept his eye on his bride as I have seen him do on less attractive-looking Germans under different circumstances, as if he were expecting her also to bolt from his custody at any moment. He faced the bearded old Ersatz Cupid, despite his alarming frock-coat and business-like quill pen, without a tremor. The 'Wedding Room' was bare of all furniture except six chairs and a green baize-covered table. A large money-box inscribed in German 'For the Poor Creatures' caused a slight misunderstanding, but Blenkins promptly restored it on my explaining that it was not in aid of himself and his bride.

"THE Ersatz Cupid reappeared, bearing a massive volume, issued, apparently, in lieu of bow and arrows. After ascertaining that Private - Soldier - of - the - British - Occupation-Army Blenkins really did wish to marry Fräulein Schneider and she him, he rather abruptly and Prussianistically pronounced the said parties to be well and truly married according to the People's Laws of the German Republic. How that last phrase must have stuck in his throat !

"THE bride, of course, signed the register wrongly, making Cupid go purple in the face. However, he recovered in time to present her with a neat little 'Householder's Book,' containing, in addition to a certificate of marriage, a great deal of Gothic print, apparently instructing her in the whole duties of the married state, including half a dozen recipes for the preparation of *sauerkraut* and sausages — at least, that's what Blenkins made of it. He himself was so overcome when Cupid unbent to offer him a congratulatory hand that he stuffed the entire paper contents of his purse into the poor-box. It took several minutes' work with a pen-knife to retrieve the ring which, in the excitement of the moment, he also presented to the poor of Cologne, after which I was relieved to see the wedding-party packed into a taxi *en route* for church and the *padre's* blessing, and to dismiss the parade."

So that, whether you like it or not, is how it's done—and will continue to be until we learn how to keep a man sober by Act of Parliament, or single by G.R.O. ERIC GORDON

SILHOUETTES BY H. L. OAKLEY
"He faced the bearded old Ersatz Cupid in a frock-coat"

'The Bystander in Occupation', 14 December 1921. (ILN/ME)

There were other acts of reconciliation too.

The first reunion dinners of the 32nd Division and the 69th Brigade were held in the Café Royal in London on consecutive evenings in May 1920, and with the same menu. Oakley designed the menu cover for the 69th Brigade around its battle honours. (JR)

This 1931 reunion was of the 23rd Division (Officers) Association. Oakley is bottom right. (JR)

Maj.-Gen. Thomas Stanton
Lambert (1871–1921).
(HLOC/ME)

After the war, Lambert gave Oakley a silver inkwell stand, inscribed:

France   Belgium   Italy   Germany
H.L.O. from T.S.L.
1916–1919

Lambert stayed in the Army after the war and served in Ireland as Colonel Commandant of the 13th Brigade based at Athlone. On the evening of 20 June 1921, he and his wife were travelling back from a tennis party with another officer and his wife in a car driven by Mrs Lambert. The car was shot at by a gang of Fenians. Lambert was hit in the neck and died shortly afterwards in hospital. The wife of the other officer was slightly injured in the face by shotgun pellets.

Accounts of events later that night vary but a common thread seems to be that a group of armed men in civilian clothes but believed to be soldiers from the nearby barracks, rampaged through the village to which they thought – apparently wrongly – that the leader of the Fenian gang had fled. They fired in the air, drove the villagers from their homes and used petrol bombs to burn out several houses.

General Lambert is buried in Brookwood military cemetery in Surrey.

Suzanne Lenglen.

Helen Wills (Moody). (HLOC/ME)

The Bystander sent Oakley to Monte Carlo and Cannes in early 1922 to cover the French season for their annual Riviera edition. He took the portrait of the French tennis player Suzanne Lenglen in Cannes, where she had probably been playing in the local tournament. Later that year she won the French singles, doubles and mixed doubles championships; a feat which she repeated twice more. Altogether she won the French and Wimbledon singles titles six times each.

Together with the American Helen Wills (later Wills Moody) they dominated ladies tennis in the 1920s; Lenglen in the first half, Wills Moody in the second. Wills Moody won the US championship six times and Wimbledon three times. They met only once, at Cannes in 1926, when Lenglen won.

(JR)

From the French Riviera to the North Wales Riviera. (JR)

When Oakley returned from Cannes he spent part of the summer of 1922 in Llandudno, which used to style itself the North Wales Riviera. He worked from a kiosk on the pier and visited the town almost every year between 1920 and his last visit in 1958. In addition to his portrait work he quickly built up a strong list of clients for his advertising work.

Chapter 10

Advertising and Promotion

The Silhouette Art of Mr. H. L. OAKLEY

is being increasingly recognised and used by National Advertisers including the following:—

The Underground
The L.&N.E. Rly.
Selfridges
Harrods
Army&Navy Stores
John Barker
Cunard Co.

'Barney's' Tobacco
Lea & Perrin
Andrews Liver Salt
Cremona Toffee
Home & Colonial S.
Fenwick's
Jenners

The attractive force of the Silhouette lies in its extreme simplicity and bold contrasts. It would indeed be difficult to find any other form of advertisement illustration which could compare with the Silhouette for sheer 'eye-catching' effect, or give the same predominance over surrounding matter.

Press Advertisements

The characterful silhouette alongside is one of a series cut by Mr. Oakley and used by Messrs. John Sinclair, Ltd., in the press advertisements of their famous tobacco—"Barney's."

Oakley's promotional card for his advertising work. (HLOC/ME)

Poster and timetable cover. (HLOC/ME)

Luggage label. (HLOC/ME)

(HLOC/ME)

L NER's continental timetables were popular with armchair travellers. The images of ferries leaving port and the details of train times and stops en route to Berlin and beyond offered the prospect of exciting journeys, even though they would never be made.

Punchbowle appeals to the *outdoor* man:

it is the "old-timer's" variety of Barney's—strong yet cool—produced for and favoured by the fresh-air loving type of man to whom a pipe-smoke means almost as much as meat and drink.

Punchbowle

3 strengths: Parsons' Pleasure is mild, Barney's itself is medium, and Punchbowle full. 1/1 the ounce throughout.

Men of Sport

have been saying nice things of Barney's ever since it travelled South—to their friends and to its makers. It is doubtful if any pipe tobacco has ever received such universal, *dis-interested* recommendation as chummy Barney's from the North Country.

Barney's

3 strengths: Parsons' Pleasure is mild, Barney's itself is medium, and Punchbowle full. 1/1 the ounce throughout.

For pipe veterans

Punchbowle is for smokers of long experience—for men who *love* the pipe; stronger than Barney's but with all its characteristic smoothness and coolness. Your 4, 6 and 8 ounces per week smoker is the type of man who smokes *and recommends* Punchbowle.

Punchbowle

3 strengths: Parsons' Pleasure is mild, Barney's itself is medium, and Punchbowle full. 1/1 the ounce throughout.

Smokers tell friends

about the cool, clean, *long-satisfying-ness* of Barney's Tobacco. Unknown outside the North Country a few short years ago, Barney's is now sold in every town and most villages throughout the land—mainly because of the recommendation from one smoker to another.

Barney's

3 strengths: Parsons' Pleasure is mild, Barney's itself is medium, and Punchbowle full. 1/1 the ounce throughout.

(HLOC/ME)

Oakley did two newspaper campaigns for John Sinclair's 'Barney's' pipe tobaccos. One of the aims was to consolidate their spread from a northern regional to a national brand.

The Children simply love sweets from

SELFRIDGE'S

SELFRIDGE & C°. LTD OXFORD ST

Books for Xmas Presents

To please all tastes
and suit all pockets

at SELFRIDGE'S

SELFRIDGE & C°. LTD OXFORD ST W.I.

(HLOC/ME)

Instinct —

the compounded lore and logic of the ages send us into the open, to exercise limbs and lungs.

Fresh air and exercise are health necessities. In the love of sport & games, we comply *instinctively* with a natural requirement for the maintenance of Health.

And because it is better to safeguard than to retrieve, fresh air, exercise *and* the occasional use of Andrews Liver Salt are fundamental in the Andrews creed of healthful living.

Andrews corrects the little Ills of Life as they arise. It effects that physical adjustment which changes of locality, weather and habit require.

Andrews is sold everywhere in the British Isles, 4 oz. tin 9d., 8 oz. tin 1/4. For the Tropics, and for Countries necessitating despatch through the Tropical Zones, Andrews is specially prepared to meet climatic changes and is supplied in bottles.

Andrews Liver Salt

Punch, 13 October 1936. (HLOC/ME)

No.1. The Landlord

No.2. The Waitress

No.3. The Head Waiter

No. 4. The Oldest Inhabitant

'Our Village in Silhouette' booklet by Worthington, Nos 1–4. (HLOC/ME)

No. 5. The Squire

No. 6. The Huntsman

No. 7. The Doctor

No. 8. The Lads of the Village

'Our Village in Silhouette' booklet by Worthington, Nos 5–8. (HLOC/ME)

A few examples of the series of advertisements now running in the sporting and farming papers —advertisements designed to help the Gunmaker and Ammunition Dealer by keeping shooting men thinking about shooting both in season and out.

ELEY=KYNOCH
CARTRIDGES

IMPERIAL CHEMICAL INDUSTRIES LTD.
MILLBANK, LONDON, S.W.1

NOBEL INDUSTRIES LIMITED

„HOLLANDIA" PATRONEN ELEY

Cal. 12 ⅝" Indian Red
Deep Shell Cartridge
geladen met

„SMOKELESS ◇ DIAMOND"
of
„E.C. 3"

„HOLLANDIA" PATRONEN

Een eerste qualiteit Engelsche jachtpatroon uitsluitend vervaardigd voor de Nederlandsche Jacht. Verkrijgbaar bij alle speciale wapenhandelaren en geweermakers

227/53/622

(HLOC/ME)

The Ely Kynoch advertisement appeared in *The Ironmonger* trade magazine in 1936.

Chapter 11

Portraiture

Self-portrait of Oakley taking the portrait of a child for the children's magazine
Peter Pan. (HLOC/ME)

Oakley in his studio in Pettigrew & Stephens, Glasgow, 1925. (HLOC/ME)

Oakley used a pair of nail scissors and paper which was black on one side and white on the other, folded white side out. Each cut therefore produced a left-facing and a right-facing portrait. He moved the paper round the scissors so that his head and the scissors remained in the same position relative to the sitter.

He cut out pieces for white patches like cuffs and collars and sometimes used white body colour for small objects or for highlights. But most of his portraits are unadorned. Auguste Edouart is said never to have used body colour or highlighting because he considered that the essence of silhouette was to capture the likeness with the outline only.

Oakley's career as a silhouettist lasted from 1913 to 1958 with a five-year gap for the war. He could cut fifty to sixty portraits a day but a conservative average would be ten to fifteen a day. If he did that for 200 days a year his annual average would be 2,500 and over a forty-year career his total output would be 100,000. That sounds a huge number but it is not implausible. Edouart is reckoned to have taken 100,000 portraits in a shorter career from the mid-1820s to the late 1840s.

Mrs St John of Bexhill, 1925.
(HLOC/ME)

Mrs Lottie Orme, 1925.
(HLOC/ME)

Mrs St John's portrait is in the Pettigrew & Stephens photograph opposite, second from the right in the bottom row.

Princess Margarita of Greece, 1926. (HLOC/ME)

Princess Theodora of Greece, 1926. (HLOC/ME)

The Greek Royal Family, 1929. Princess Margarita is sitting left. Princess Theodora is sitting right. The boy in the sailor suit is Prince Philip, the Duke of Edinburgh. (The Royal Collection/© Her Majesty Queen Elizabeth II, 2013)

David Lloyd George. (NPG)

Gustav Holst. (NPG)

This portrait of Lloyd George was taken in Llandudno, a few miles from Caernarvon, which he represented in Parliament for fifty-five years from 1890 to 1945.

When the First World War started Holst had wanted to enlist but failed the medical. He had already begun his *Planets Suite* with the foreboding tones of *Mars, the Bringer of War*, and he was thus able to continue to work on the suite. It was finished in 1916 but not performed with a full orchestra until after the war.

Lord Provost Thomson of Edinburgh.
(HLOC/ME)

Burns Esq. of Edinburgh.
(HLOC/ME)

SILHOUETTE
PORTRAITS

100 YEARS AGO.

From the " Scotsman " of Saturday, 13th February, 1830.

" Patronized by His Royal Highness the Duke of Gloucester. Monsieur Edouart, Silhouettiste, from Paris, Princes Street, opposite the Mound, respectfully invites the Nobility and Gentry to his Public Exhibition (Gratis) with upwards of 30,000 Silhouette Likenesses of some of the first Characters in England, who have honoured him with a sitting at London, Cheltenham, Bath, Oxford, Cambridge, Eton, &c. Mr Edouart produces, in a manner peculiar to himself, without other aid than that of the scissors, correct likenesses, in a few minutes, by which the expression of the Passions and peculiarity of character are portrayed in a style which has not hitherto been attempted by any other Artist."

Many of EDOUART'S Silhouettes of Famous Scottish Personages are to day in the Scottish National Portrait Gallery.

TO-DAY.

JENNER'S have pleasure in intimating that they have arranged with the well-known Silhouette Artist,

Mr H. L. OAKLEY, M.B.E.,

to cut portraits daily in their BAZAAR DEPARTMENT during the next few weeks.

Mr Oakley, whose work was a regular feature of the " Bystander " during the War, has been given sittings by H.R.H. The Prince of Wales and many other prominent people. He works without any previous drawing, cutting all his portraits direct from the sitters while they wait.

Mr Oakley's Silhouettes of Children are particularly successful in full-length portraits, forming very novel and lasting Christmas gifts when framed in " passe partout."

Fees are from **2/6** for two copies.

JENNER'S
PRINCES·STREET
EDINBURGH

Jenner's department store in Edinburgh was a favourite Christmas location.
(HLOC/ME)

A London Sketch Club Smoker. Oakley is the vicar. (HLOC/ME)

Oakley was a long-time member of the London Sketch Club and spent a lot of time there when he was in London. As well as promoting the art of sketching, the club had a very strong social side and was an ideal place for a bachelor artist to go in the evenings. There were weekly sketching sessions followed by supper, life classes, smoker nights, ladies' nights, an annual exhibition of members' work and for some years an annual dance. Most members were graphic artists or cartoonists working for London newspapers and magazines. The club had more than its share of 'characters' and the atmosphere at times was said to border on the Bohemian.

As well as being a good place to relax it was also a good place for Oakley to work. His silhouette portraits took only a few minutes – they were essentially sketches – so he took many portraits of fellow members during the sketching sessions. He was president of the club in its Golden Jublilee year 1947–48.

There is a frieze of silhouette portraits of distinguished members, including Oakley, around the top of the clubhouse walls. The frieze is on demountable panels and where the club goes the frieze goes too. The clubhouse today is in Chelsea.

Some of Studdy's cartoons were published in *The Bystander* but most of his work was done for the *Sketch*, where he created Bonzo the dog which became enormously popular. As well as the *Sketch*, Bonzo appeared in magazines, books, films and on postcards, toys, games, china and many other items.

George Studdy. (NPG)

H.M. Bateman. (NPG)

W. Heath Robinson. (NPG)

Bateman and Heath Robinson were colleagues of Oakley at *The Bystander*, as well as fellow members of the Sketch Club. Bateman is remembered for his 'The man who …' cartoons showing a cringing man being bawled out for some faux pas. Heath Robinson's name is still in the dictionary today for his over-ingenious mechanical contrivances.

Unknown ladies middle/late 1930s. (HLOC/ME)

Three children. (HLOC/ME)

Chapter 12

War and Peace Again

Polish officer, Edinburgh, 1943. (HLOC/ME)

Oakley's portraits were again popular with servicemen and women during the Second World War.

Second World War portraits. (HLOC/ME)

8th Air Force (Detroit) (top left); USA WAAC (top right); Lt RNR (bottom left); and Scots Guard (bottom right).

(HLOC/ME)

Second World War portraits.

(JR)

Burmah (top left); 8th Air Force (Massachusetts) (top right); Captain
Garrelt QMC USA (bottom left); and ATS (bottom right).

Second World War portraits. (HLOC/ME)

Wren officer (Women's Royal Naval Service); WRAC (Women's Royal Army Corps); and Lieutenant RN (Royal Navy).

Land Girl, Edinburgh, 1943.
(HLOC/ME)

Second Lieutenant Black Watch.
(HLOC/ME)

'The Horse at War', *Holly Leaves*, 1941. (ILN/ME)

After the Second World War, Oakley concentrated on his portraits and a few large pieces like this one for *Holly Leaves*, 1948. (© ILN/ME)

Holly Leaves, 1949. (ILN/ME)

A Savage Club golf day, early 1950s. (HLOC/ME)

Oakley is standing second from the right. The film actor Jack Hawkins is sixth from the right.

Oakley was a keen golfer. In Llandudno he was a member of one of the local clubs and played in club competitions. When in London he went on golf days organised by the Savage Club of which he was also a member.

Oakley's last published piece for *Holly Leaves*, 1957. (ILN/ME)

Oakley outside his kiosk on the pier at Llandudno, 1957. (HLOC/ME)

Oakley's last visit to Llandudno was in the summer of 1958. He died after a stroke in London on 17 January 1960 and was cremated at Golders Green crematorium. His ashes are interred in St Tudno's churchyard high up on the Great Orme. A memorial stone a few yards outside the west door reads:

Oakley, Harry Lawrence, MBE, ARCA.
Captain 8th Yorkshire Regiment, The Green Howards.
Artist and Silhouettist. Of York and Salop.

(HLOC/ME)

Index

Silhouette Portraits by H.L. Oakley

If you enjoyed this book, you may also be interested in…

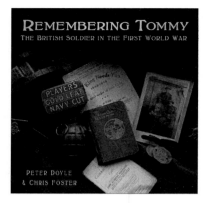

Remembering Tommy: The British Soldier in the First World War

PETER DOYLE & CHRIS FOSTER

Remembering Tommy pays tribute to the real-life British soldier of the Great War. How did the soldier live, where did he sleep? What was it like to go over the top, and when he did, what did he carry with him? In stunning new images of uniforms, equipment and ephemera, it conjures the atmosphere of the trenches through the belongings of the soldiers themselves – allowing us to almost reach out and touch history.

978 0 7524 7955 2

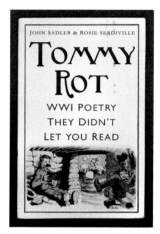

Tommy Rot: WWI Poetry They Didn't Let You Read

JOHN SADLER & ROSIE SERDIVILLE

Tommy Rot is a never-before-published collection of humorous and un-jingoistic war poetry from the trench and front line. Many of the poems have never been seen in print before and come almost entirely from archives. Offering a unique insight and a different approach leading up to the 1914 centenary, each poem is accompanied by a brief background on the author and campaign.

978 0 7524 9208 7

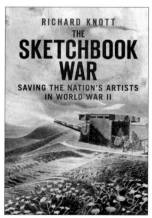

The Sketchbook War: Saving the Nation's Artists in World War II

RICHARD KNOTT

The Sketchbook War is not a book about art but the story of war artists; how men who had previously made a comfortable living painting in studios were transformed by military uniforms and experiences that were to shape the rest of their lives and the way in which we view war today. Richard Knott follows the experiences of eight artists who formed a close bond on the front line, and demonstrates how war and art came together in a moving and dramatic way.

978 0 7524 8923 0

Visit our website and discover thousands of other History Press books.

www.thehistorypress.co.uk